Green Mountain Grill Davy Crockett Grill & Smoker Cookbook

The Ultimate Guide to Master Your Green Mountain Grill with Flavorful Recipes for the Tastiest Barbecue

Kantien Brardon

© Copyright 2020 Kantien Brardon - All Rights Reserved.

In no way is it legal to reproduce, duplicate, or transmit any part of this document by either electronic means or in printed format. Recording of this publication is strictly prohibited, and any storage of this material is not allowed unless with written permission from the publisher. All rights reserved.

The information provided herein is stated to be truthful and consistent, in that any liability, regarding inattention or otherwise, by any usage or abuse of any policies, processes, or directions contained within is the solitary and complete responsibility of the recipient reader. Under no circumstances will any legal liability or blame be held against the publisher for any reparation, damages, or monetary loss due to the information herein, either directly or indirectly.

Respective authors own all copyrights not held by the publisher.

Legal Notice:

This book is copyright protected. This is only for personal use. You cannot amend, distribute, sell, use, quote or paraphrase any part of the content within this book without the consent of the author or copyright owner. Legal action will be pursued if this is breached.

Disclaimer Notice:

Please note the information contained within this document is for educational and entertainment purposes only. Every attempt has been made to provide accurate, up-to-date and reliable, complete information. No warranties of any kind are expressed or implied. Readers acknowledge that the author is not engaging in the rendering of legal, financial, medical or professional advice.

By reading this document, the reader agrees that under no circumstances are we responsible for any losses, direct or indirect, which are incurred as a result of the use of information contained within this document, including, but not limited to, errors, omissions, or inaccuracies.

Table of Contents

Introduction 7
Chapter 1: Grilling Made Easy 8
    History of Green Mountain Grills 8
    What is Green Mountain Davy Crockett Wood Pellet Grill? 8
    Features of Green Mountain Davy Crockett Wood Pellet Grill? 9
Chapter 2: Breakfast 12
    Bacon and Egg Bites 12
    Grilled Quiche 14
    Breakfast Cheese Sandwiches 15
    Eggs on the Grill 17
    Breakfast Sausage 18
Chapter 3: Poultry 19
    Chicken Thighs 19
    Herb and Beer Chicken 20
    Sriracha, Honey and Lime Drumsticks 22
    Citrus Herb Grilled Chicken 24
    Fried Chicken 25
    Chicken and Bacon Ranch Pizza 27
    Miami Chicken Wings 28
    Cilantro Wings 30
Chapter 4: Games 32
    Rice Stuffed Game Hens 32
    Whole Turkey 33
    Duck 35
    Honey and Jalapeno Turkey 36

Venison Poppers 38

Venison Ham 39

Venison Steak 41

Chapter 5: Beef **42**

Spiced Beef Long Ribs 42

Meat Log 44

Meatballs 46

Stuffed Meatballs 47

Smoked Tri-Tip 48

Black Pepper Smoked Jerky 49

Steaks 50

Beef Brisket 51

BBQ Burger 53

Smoked Prime Rib 54

Brats 55

Chapter 6: Pork **56**

Pork Belly Burnt Ends 56

Beer Brats 58

Cherry Chipotle Ribs 59

Sweet Espresso Ribs 60

BBQ Pulled Pork 61

Baby Back Ribs 63

Pork Chops 64

Chapter 7: Lamb **65**

Mustard Glazed Lamb 65

Lamb Kabob 67

    Rack of Lamb 69

Chapter 8: Seafood and Fish **70**
    Pineapple and Coconut Shrimp 70
    Spicy Shrimp Skewers 72
    Bacon-Wrapped Shrimp 74
    Shrimp Chipotle 75
    Smoked Salmon 76
    Basic Fish 78
    Salmon Steaks 80
    Catfish Fillets 81
    Grilled Whole Trout 82
    Grilled Tilapia 84
    Grilled Seabass 85

Chapter 9: Vegetables **86**
    Parmesan and Kale Pizza 86
    Watermelon Gazpacho 87
    Baked Beans 88
    Corn on the Cob 90
    Vegetable Medley 91
    Potato Wedges 92
    Vegetables and Mozzarella Bowl 93

Chapter 10: Sides and Snacks **95**
    Citrus Mimosa 95
    Jalapeno Poppers 96
    Tomato and Bacon Jalapeno Poppers 97
    Cilantro and Lime Grilled Corn 99

Potatoes with Rosemary and Paprika	101
Chapter 11: Desserts	**102**
Banana Boats	102
Grilled Fruit Skewers	103
Grilled Peaches	104
Chocolate Chip Cookies	105
Pineapple with Nutella	106
Blackberry Crisp	107
Conclusion	**109**

Introduction

Can't find the grill that serves your every need?

Do you want a compatible and easy to use a grill to fulfill your hunger for barbeques and steaks?

Then Green Mountain's Davy Crockett might be for you. Before buying anything, you need to know every available option on the market and choose the one that serves your needs best. You might want something big to serve huge backyard parties. You may just want a grill for personal use in your apartment. Depending on your requirements, you make a purchase and hope that it goes further with its features.

Wood pellets grills are trending nowadays. There are many advantages to them, but the major one is that it brings more flavor to your meats. You can't impress a barbeque enthusiast with a gas grill anymore. They know that the most efficient option is the wood pellet grills. If you want to taste the best steaks at home, you would want to get this grill instead of old fashion gas. This product gives you a wood pallet grill at a low price so that you taste the difference yourself.

One of the major concerns about getting a grill is that they are very heavy and too big for someone who doesn't have a lawn or a backyard. Does that mean people living in small spaces can't enjoy grilling at home? Not at all! With the introduction of portable grills, you can have a grill party even at your apartment without much worry. If you are going for portable, then the best product for you is this Davy Crockett Grill.

If you're an outdoors person and want to use your grill to different campsites and open lands, then this device's portability also comes in handy. Moreover, you don't need an additional power inverter as this grill work without the need for it. There is no better product out there to create the best outdoor grilling experience. With minimal effort and little expense, you can create unique moments with friends and families.

Nowadays, almost the product has become 'Smart.' By 'smart,' I mean the ability to be controlled by your phone via Bluetooth or Wi-Fi. This way, you can operate key functions of the device without even getting up from your couch. Davy Crockett Grill comes with this convenient feature. It brings more flexibility in cooking. You can multitask and still be able to make the perfect meals. The world of the grill is moving forward with the world's technology so that you fully enjoy your grilling days.

Chapter 1: Grilling Made Easy

History of Green Mountain Grills

People that started Green Mountain Grills were grilling fanatics that wanted to improve on the grills that were available at the time. The company started in 2006, and since then, it has gained much popularity and attention from the grilling community. The company started advertising their grills as having an 'Open Flame technology.' The grills used to come with two drip pans, but this has now been discontinued. Since 2018, the grills now come with a single, big drip pan. The Open Flame option is still available if anybody wants to use it. This was a strategy taken to improve the grill's portability and function. The company has come up a long way, winning many awards, including 2013 VESTA for 'Barbecues, Other Fuel' for this particular device " Davy Crockett'. The device also earned a 'Best Value Gold medal' at Amazingribs.com. The Green Mountain Grill company has been dealing with the manufacturing and selling of different household electrical and non-electrical cooking equipment up till now.

What is Green Mountain Davy Crockett Wood Pellet Grill?

Green Mountain Davy Crockett Wood Pellet Grill is a choice for small families who want to enjoy a few ribs and steaks. If you are a tailgater, a camper, live in an RV or a small apartment, or generally like cooking outside, then this product gives the best value for your buck.

It is very convenient. Sit at the couch and adjust your temperature settings with precision. Its Wi-Fi capability and the 'Smart' app make this task possible. Set the temperature between 150F to 550F degrees with precise 5F degree differences.

This device is the go-to portable grill for many people. It is 68 pounds in weight and can be easily placed in the back of any car, which makes a great grill for tailgating and all other people who need to grill outside. Its smart app is available on both systems IOS and Android. You will be able to monitor your grill's temperature from anywhere in the range of the WI-FI connection. It has a built-in meat probe that can check the internal temperature of the meat. It also comes with a convenience tray with hooked utensils and a peaked lid for rib racks. The temperature is sensed through a device in the grill called Sense-Mate. This is the thermal sensor that precisely judges the temperature of flames. The temperature is shown on a LED display or your phone. This grill can be hooked onto a wall outlet with 120AC supply and also to a car cigarette outlet with 12V DC supply.

Grill Functionality:

Below the pallet placing box (the Hopper), there is a motor which, when turned on, makes the auger feed the wood pellets to the firebox. The firebox is automatically ignited when turned on by a hot rod. Just below the hot rod, a combustion fan, to feed air into the firebox. There are vertical vents present at the level of the firebox so that the fire keeps burning. The smoke of the wood is circulated throughout the grill. The chimney needs to be open wide when using to let the smoke escape.

Technical Specs:

- The minimum voltage required is 12V
- The minimum Wattage required is 60W average.
- Weight is around 57 lbs.
- The dimensions of the wood pallet when open legs are 31.75" H x 34" W x 23" D
- The dimensions of the wood pallet when closed legs are 20.5" H x 27.75" W x 17.5" D
- The surface area of the grill is 219 square inches.
- The motor of the auger is around 5 RPM
- The motor of the fan is around 0.45A; 4100 RPM
- The grease tray is made up of 13-gauge steel.
- The grease tray function revolves around Open Flame Technology.
- The igniter produces 12 volt and 100 watts.
- The distance between the lead and the cooking surface is approximate 7.7 inches
- The Hopper has a capacity of 9 LBS of pallets.

Features of Green Mountain Davy Crockett Wood Pellet Grill?

- 12-volt direct power

For making outdoor grilling more efficient, the device comes with a 12-volt direct power outlet. This gives a greater economy of electricity and pallet use. It also promotes fast startups.

- Digital Controller

With just buttons and knobs, you can control the temperature precisely by 5 degree F differences. It has smart control and also a USB charging port.

- Auger system

The micro-adjust variable speed fan is attached to the auger. This gives feeding the firebox at a constant speed, in which efficient Oxygen and pallets are supplied.

- Pallet Hopper

With an 18 LBS capacity of pallets, it feeds the hot firebox for a long-time. It also has a window so you can check consumption and an easy to remove door at the back for optimum cleaning. It also has a bottle opener placed on it.

- Wi-Fi smart control

Monitor and control the internal temperature of your food from anywhere within the range of the Wi-Fi. You can also access unlimited recipes and grilling profiles. The temperature can be changed precisely by the degree on your phone.

- The firebox

The firebox is designed to minimize waste and maximize the efficiency of the pallets. The Venturi style design of the works makes for maximum distribution of heat. It creates a hot pot where the air is circulated all around.

- Benefits of Wood Pellet Grilling

Wood pellet grills are becoming more popular nowadays. Charcoal and gas are becoming obsolete day by day and are being replaced by these grills. It is because they provide a large variety of advantages that fulfills everyone's grilling needs. Some advantages of the grill are listed below:

- It is versatile

This is one of the major benefits. You can prepare a large variety of delicious food with just one device. You can roast chicken breasts and braise short ribs without much hassle.

- It is fast

Everything is becoming fast and efficient, so why not grilling. Wood pellet grills save a lot of time because they circulate heat quickly. The grill gets preheated fast as well. People cook faster using these grills with ease.

- It is good at regulating internal temperature

A perfect cooking experience calls for perfect control of the internal temperature of the meat. Charcoal and gas can have fluctuating internal temperatures, which are not easy to control. This gives you meats with the optimum flavor

- They give out more even heat

Charcoal and gas have a problem of fluctuating temperatures, and they are very hard to control. With wood pellet grills, the meat is cooked evenly without much flipping over or moving around on the grill. These grills provide you with the heat diffuser plate, in which you can put hardwood chips for a better smoke.

- It is more customizable

These grills are sold in different shapes and sizes, catering to every individual's needs. Several specific features are added to different grills that appeal to the wants of different people.

- It provides more flavoring

If the grill machine itself gives a hand to elevate the flavor, then itself that machine is worth more than others. By using different wood pellets, you can give distinct flavors to your meats. Some flavors include maple, pecan, and apple.

- It is safer to use and give less smoke

In a traditional grill, you had to use your hands to adjust the heat directly. Wood pellet grills are electrically controlled grills that don't need you to go anywhere near the flame. The smoke generated is also less in amount and controlled.

Chapter 2: Breakfast

Bacon and Egg Bites

Preparation time: 10 minutes
Cooking time: 1 hour
Servings: 6

Ingredients:

- 1 pound of bacon slices
- 4 tablespoons chopped cilantro
- 1 medium red bell pepper, cored, minced
- 1 medium white onion, peeled, minced
- 1 cup minced shiitake mushrooms
- 1 tablespoon salt
- 1 tablespoon ground black pepper
- 1 tablespoon poultry rub
- 2 tablespoons butter, unsalted
- 6 eggs, at room temperature
- 1 cup grated parmesan cheese

Method:

1. Take a medium saucepan, place it over medium heat, add butter and when it melts, add mushroom, pepper, and onion, and then stir until poultry rub.
2. Bring the mixture to simmer, continue cooking the mixture until vegetables have turned soft, and then set aside until cooled.
3. Then switch on the grill, go to the WiFi setting on your cell phone, and then connect with the grill by using your serial number as the password.
4. Go to the app of Green Mountain Grill, press the 'connect' button, and when connected, go to its setting and select the WiFi mode option and after few minutes, select the connect option again.
5. Prepare the grill, and for this, fill it hopper with gold blend wood pallets, go to Green Mountain Grill app, set the grill temperature to 400 degrees F, and let it preheat.
6. When the grill has preheated, open its lid, place bacon slices on the grilling mat and then grill until almost edible.
7. Then remove bacon slices from the grill, let them cool for 5 minutes and then wipe clean the grease from the mat.
8. Chop the bacon, add to the cooked vegetable mixture, then add cheese, stir until well combined, and then divide the mixture evenly among six muffin tins.

9. Crack an egg into each muffin cup, sprinkle with salt, black pepper and cilantro, place the muffin cups on the grilling, and then grill at 300 degrees F for 50 minutes until eggs have set.
10. When done, let egg bites cool for 5 minutes, and then serve.

Nutrition Value:

- Calories: 310 Cal
- Fat: 22 g
- Carbs: 9 g
- Protein: 19 g
- Fiber: 2 g

Grilled Quiche

Preparation time: 10 minutes
Cooking time: 1 hour and 30 minutes
Servings: 4

Ingredients:

- 1 pie crust, pre-made
- ½ cup all-purpose flour
- 1 tablespoon sugar
- 1 teaspoon baking powder
- 3 ounces cream cheese, softened
- ¼ cup butter, unsalted
- 2 cups cottage cheese, cream-style
- 6 eggs, at room temperature, beaten
- 1 cup skim milk, unsweetened
- 1 pound Monterey jack cheese

Method:

1. Take a medium saucepan over medium heat, add butter and when it melts, whisk in flour until the thick and smooth mixture comes together.
2. Cook the mixture for 3 to 5 minutes until golden, and then whisk in sugar, baking powder, beaten eggs, milk, cream cheese, and cottage cheese until well combined.
3. Then switch on the grill, go to the WiFi setting on your cell phone, and then connect with the grill by using your serial number as the password.
4. Go to the app of Green Mountain Grill, press the 'connect' button, and when connected, go to its setting and select the WiFi mode option and after few minutes, select the connect option again.
5. Prepare the grill, and for this, fill it hopper with gold blend wood pallets, go to Green Mountain Grill app, set the grill temperature to 350 degrees F, and let it preheat.
6. Meanwhile, place the pie crust into the 9-by-13 disposable aluminum tray, pour in the cooked filling, and then top with Monterey Jack cheese cubes.
7. When the grill has preheated, open its lid, place prepared quiche on the pellet grill, shut with lid and let it grill for 1 hour or 1 hour and 15 minutes until quiche has set and inserted knife in the center of the quiche comes out clean.
8. When done, let the quiche rest for 10 minutes, cut it into slices and then serve.

Nutrition Value:

- Calories: 877.8 Cal
- Fat: 69 g
- Carbs: 25.5 g
- Protein: 38 g
- Fiber: 1 g

Breakfast Cheese Sandwiches

Preparation time: 10 minutes
Cooking time: 20 minutes
Servings: 2

Ingredients:

- 4 slices of white bread
- 6 strips of cooked bacon
- 1/8 teaspoon salt
- 1/8 teaspoon ground black pepper
- 1 tablespoon butter, unsalted
- 1 tablespoon milk
- 4 eggs, at room temperature
- 4 slices of Colby cheddar cheese

Method:

1. Prepare the eggs, and for this, crack the eggs in a large bowl, add salt, black pepper, and milk and then whisk until blended.
2. Take a large skillet pan, place it over medium heat, add butter and when it melts, pour in the egg mixture.
3. Spread egg mixture in the pan, let it cook for 3 minutes per side until evenly cooked, and then transfer to a plate.
4. Switch on the grill, go to the WiFi setting on your cell phone, and then connect with the grill by using your serial number as the password.
5. Go to the app of Green Mountain Grill, press the 'connect' button, and when connected, go to its setting and select the WiFi mode option and after few minutes, select the connect option again.
6. Prepare the grill, and for this, fill it hopper with gold blend wood pallets, go to Green Mountain Grill app, set the grill temperature to 400 degrees F, and let it preheat.
7. Meanwhile, assemble the sandwiches, and for this, place a cheese slice on two slices of bread, top evenly with eggs and slices with bacon.
8. Cover with the remaining cheese slices, top with the remaining bread slices, and then spread bread on the exposed side of sandwiches.
9. When the grill has preheated, open its lid, place the sandwiches on the pellet grill, shut with lid and let it grill for 4 to 5 minutes per side until cheese melts and grill marks appear on the sandwich
10. Serve straight away.

Nutrition Value:

- Calories: 340 Cal
- Fat: 19 g
- Carbs: 26 g
- Protein: 15.6 g
- Fiber: 3 g

Eggs on the Grill

Preparation time: 5 minutes
Cooking time: 5 minutes
Servings: 8

Ingredients:

- 8 eggs, on room temperature
- Salt as needed
- Ground black pepper as needed

Method:

1. Switch on the grill, go to the WiFi setting on your cell phone, and then connect with the grill by using your serial number as the password.
2. Go to the app of Green Mountain Grill, press the 'connect' button, and when connected, go to its setting and select the WiFi mode option and after few minutes, select the connect option again.
3. Prepare the grill, and for this, fill it hopper with gold blend wood pallets, go to Green Mountain Grill app, set the grill temperature to 450 degrees F, and let it preheat.
4. Meanwhile, take a muffin tray of eight cups, grease it with oil, and then crack an egg in each cup.
5. When the grill has preheated, open its lid, place muffin on the pellet grill by using a tong, shut with lid, and let it grill for 3 to 5 minutes until eggs have cooked to the desired doneness.
6. When done, sprinkle salt and black pepper on eggs and then serve.

Nutrition Value:

- Calories: 90 Cal
- Fat: 9.9 g
- Carbs: 0.8 g
- Protein: 12.6 g
- Fiber: 0 g

Breakfast Sausage

Preparation time: 10 minutes
Cooking time: 20 minutes
Servings: 6

Ingredients:

- 1-pound breakfast sausage links, at room temperature
- 1 tablespoon Dijon mustard
- ½ cup apricot jam

Method:

1. Switch on the grill, go to the WiFi setting on your cell phone, and then connect with the grill by using your serial number as the password.
2. Go to the app of Green Mountain Grill, press the 'connect' button, and when connected, go to its setting and select the WiFi mode option and after few minutes, select the connect option again.
3. Prepare the grill, and for this, fill it hopper with gold blend wood pallets, go to Green Mountain Grill app, set the grill temperature to 350 degrees F, and let it preheat.
4. Meanwhile, prepare the glaze, and for this, take a small saucepan, place it over low heat, pour in apricot jam and mustard, stir until mixed and then cook for 3 to 5 minutes until warmed, set aside until required.
5. When the grill has preheated, open its lid, place sausages on the pellet grill by using a tong, shut with lid, and let it grill for 15 minutes, turning every 5 minutes.
6. Then brush each sausage with the apricot jam mixture, return sausages on the grill and continue grilling for 2 to 3 minutes until glazed.
7. Serve straight away.

Nutrition Value:

- Calories: 283 Cal
- Fat: 25 g
- Carbs: 2.4 g
- Protein: 12 g

Chapter 3: Poultry

Chicken Thighs

Preparation time: 10 minutes
Cooking time: 30 minutes
Servings: 6

Ingredients:

- 3 pounds chicken thighs, skinless, at room temperature
- 2 tablespoons poultry rub
- ½ of lemon, juiced
- 1/3 cup yellow mustard
- ½ cup sweet BBQ sauce

Method:

1. Marinade the chicken, and for this, take a large plastic bag, place chicken thighs in it, and then add remaining ingredients.
2. Seal the bag, turn it upside down to coat the chicken with the ingredients, and then marinate them for a minimum of 2 hours or 6 hours in the refrigerator.
3. When ready to grill, switch on the grill, go to the WiFi setting on your cell phone, and then connect with the grill by using your serial number as the password.
4. Go to the app of Green Mountain Grill, press the 'connect' button, and when connected, go to its setting and select the WiFi mode option and after few minutes, select the connect option again.
5. Prepare the grill, and for this, fill it hopper with gold blend wood pallets, go to Green Mountain Grill app, set the grill temperature to 420 degrees F, and let it preheat.
6. When the grill has preheated, open its lid, place chicken thighs on the pellet grill by using a tong, and then grill for 15 minutes per side until the marinade over chicken begins to caramelize.
7. When grilled, transfer the chicken thighs to a dish, let it rest for 10 minutes, and then serve.

Nutrition Value:

- Calories: 124.5 Cal
- Fat: 2.7 g
- Carbs: 10.6 g
- Protein: 13.6 g
- Fiber: 0 g

Herb and Beer Chicken

Preparation time: 10 minutes
Cooking time: 2 hours and 30 minutes
Servings: 6

Ingredients:

- 1 whole chicken, cleaned, rinsed, at room temperature
- 2 teaspoons minced garlic
- 1 tablespoon salt
- 2 teaspoons chopped thyme
- 1 tablespoon ground black pepper
- 2 teaspoons chopped dill
- 1 tablespoon chopped rosemary
- 2 tablespoons olive oil
- 1 can of beer, empty

Method:

1. Switch on the grill, go to the WiFi setting on your cell phone, and then connect with the grill by using your serial number as the password.
2. Go to the app of Green Mountain Grill, press the 'connect' button, and when connected, go to its setting and select the WiFi mode option and after few minutes, select the connect option again.
3. Prepare the grill, and for this, fill it hopper with apple blend wood pallets, go to Green Mountain Grill app, set the grill temperature to 350 degrees F, and let it preheat.
4. Meanwhile, prepare the chicken, and for this, rub the exterior of chicken with olive.
5. Take a small bowl, add all the seasonings and herbs, stir until mixed, and then sprinkle this mixture all over the chicken until evenly coated.
6. Take an empty beer can and then place the prepared chicken on it, inserting the can in the chicken as much as possible.
7. When the grill has preheated, open its lid, place chicken on the pellet grill by using a tong, shut with lid and let it grill for 2 to 2 hours and 30 minutes or set the food temperature to 165 degrees F in the app and let it grill until the food reaches the set food temperature.
8. Once the app shows that the internal temperature of the chicken has reached 165 degrees F, open the grill and then transfer chicken to a dish.
9. Remove can from the chicken, let it rest for 10 minutes, then carve the chicken into pieces and serve.

Nutrition Value:

- Calories: 161 Cal
- Fat: 6.3 g
- Carbs: 0.2 g
- Protein: 25 g
- Fiber: 0.1 g

Sriracha, Honey and Lime Drumsticks

Preparation time: 10 minutes
Cooking time: 2 hours and 20 minutes
Servings: 4

Ingredients:

- 4 pounds chicken drumsticks, at room temperature
- 4 teaspoons minced garlic
- 2 teaspoon salt
- 2 tablespoons melted butter, unsalted

For the Sauce:

- 1 tablespoon chopped cilantro
- 2 tablespoons honey
- 1 tablespoon lime juice
- ½ cup Sriracha sauce
- 1 ½ tablespoons soy sauce
- 1 teaspoon rice vinegar
- 4 tablespoons melted butter

Method:

1. Switch on the grill, go to the WiFi setting on your cell phone, and then connect with the grill by using your serial number as the password.
2. Go to the app of Green Mountain Grill, press the 'connect' button, and when connected, go to its setting and select the WiFi mode option and after few minutes, select the connect option again.
3. Prepare the grill, and for this, fill it hopper with gold blend wood pallets, go to Green Mountain Grill app, set the grill temperature to 250 degrees F, and let it preheat.
4. Meanwhile, take a large bowl, place chicken drumsticks in it, add garlic, salt and butter and then mix until well coated.
5. Prepare the sauce, and for this, take a small pan, place it over low heat, add butter and when it melts, whisk in remaining ingredients and then cook for 2 minutes.
6. When the grill has preheated, open its lid, place chicken on the pellet grill by using a tong.
7. Brush chicken prepared sauce, shut with lid, and then let it grill for 2 hours.
8. Then transfer chicken drumsticks to a cutting board, brush again with the sauce, return chicken to the grill and continue grilling for 20 minutes until crispy.
9. When done, transfer chicken drumsticks to a dish, cover with the remaining sauce and then serve.

Nutrition Value:

- Calories: 121.2 Cal
- Fat: 3.3 g
- Carbs: 15.5 g
- Protein: 8.1 g
- Fiber: 0.1 g

Citrus Herb Grilled Chicken

Preparation time: 10 minutes
Cooking time: 30 minutes
Servings: 4

Ingredients:

- 4 chicken breasts, at room temperature
- 1 medium red onion, peeled, minced
- 2 ½ teaspoons minced garlic
- 1 cup chopped cilantro
- 1 teaspoon salt
- 1 tablespoon ground black pepper
- 3 lemons, juiced
- ¼ cup olive oil

Method:

1. Prepare the marinade, and for this, place onion in it, add remaining ingredients except for chicken and then stir until combined.
2. Add chicken, toss until chicken has well coated, and then marinate it for a minimum of 2 hours in the refrigerator.
3. When ready to grill, switch on the grill, go to the WiFi setting on your cell phone, and then connect with the grill by using your serial number as the password.
4. Go to the app of Green Mountain Grill, press the 'connect' button, and when connected, go to its setting and select the WiFi mode option and after few minutes, select the connect option again.
5. Prepare the grill, and for this, fill it hopper with gold blend wood pallets, go to Green Mountain Grill app, set the grill temperature to 425 degrees F, and let it preheat.
6. When the grill has preheated, open its lid, place chicken breasts on the pellet grill by using a tong, shut with lid and let it grill for 15 minutes per side or set the food temperature to 165 degrees F in the app and let it grill until the food reaches the set food temperature, flipping the chicken halfway.
7. Once the app shows that the internal temperature of the chicken has reached 165 degrees F, open the grill, and then transfer the chicken breasts to a dish.
8. Let the chicken rest for 10 minutes, then cut it into slices and serve.

Nutrition Value:

- Calories: 380 Cal
- Fat: 8 g
- Carbs: 6 g
- Protein: 67 g
- Fiber: 1 g

Fried Chicken

Preparation time: 10 minutes
Cooking time: 55 minutes
Servings: 4

Ingredients:

- 1 whole chicken, cleaned, rinsed, cut-up for frying
- ¾ cup all-purpose flour
- 1 tablespoon baking powder
- ½ teaspoon salt
- ½ teaspoon ground black pepper
- ½ teaspoon seasoned salt
- 1 tablespoon paprika
- 1/3 cup evaporated milk
- 1 egg

Method:

1. Switch on the grill, go to the WiFi setting on your cell phone, and then connect with the grill by using your serial number as the password.
2. Go to the app of Green Mountain Grill, press the 'connect' button, and when connected, go to its setting and select the WiFi mode option and after few minutes, select the connect option again.
3. Prepare the grill, and for this, fill it hopper with gold blend wood pallets, go to Green Mountain Grill app, set the grill temperature to 375 degrees F, and let it preheat.
4. Meanwhile, prepare the chicken, and for this, take a shallow dish, crack the egg in it, beat it, and then beat in milk until incorporated.
5. Take a shallow dish, place flour in it and then stir in salt, seasoned salt, black pepper, paprika, and baking powder.
6. Dip each chicken piece in egg-milk mixture, dredge in flour mixture and then arrange it onto butter greased baking pan.
7. When the grill has preheated, open its lid, place baking pan containing chicken pieces on the pellet grill, shut with lid, grill the chicken for 25 minutes, then switch temperature to 325 degrees F and continue grilling the chicken for 30 minutes or more until done.
8. When done, transfer fried chicken to a dish, let it rest for 10 minutes, and then serve.

Nutrition Value:

- Calories: 192 Cal
- Fat: 7.6 g
- Carbs: 2 g
- Protein: 28 g
- Fiber: 1 g

Chicken and Bacon Ranch Pizza

Preparation time: 15 minutes
Cooking time: 5 minutes
Servings: 4

Ingredients:

- 1 pizza crust, at room temperature
- ½ cup shredded chicken
- 4 ounces smoked bacon
- 2 green onions, sliced
- 1 medium white onion, peeled, sliced
- 1 medium green bell pepper, destemmed, cored, peeled, sliced
- 1/3 cup ranch dressing
- ¾ cup shredded mozzarella cheese

Method:

1. Switch on the grill, go to the WiFi setting on your cell phone, and then connect with the grill by using your serial number as the password.
2. Go to the app of Green Mountain Grill, press the 'connect' button, and when connected, go to its setting and select the WiFi mode option and after few minutes, select the connect option again.
3. Prepare the grill, and for this, fill it hopper with gold blend wood pallets, go to Green Mountain Grill app, set the grill temperature to 350 degrees F, and let it preheat.
4. Meanwhile, prepare the pizza, and for this, take a pizza peel, spread cornmeal on it and then transfer pizza crust on it.
5. Spread ranch dressing on the crust, spread chicken, bacon, onion, green onion, and bell pepper on top and then cover with cheese.
6. When the grill has preheated, open its lid, place pizza on the pellet grill, shut with lid and let it grill for 5 minutes or until cheese melts and crust have turned golden brown.
7. When done, remove prepared pizza from the grill, let it rest for 2 minutes on the pizza peel and then cut it into eight slices.
8. Serve straight away.

Nutrition Value:

- Calories: 416 Cal
- Fat: 20 g
- Carbs: 37 g
- Protein: 21 g
- Fiber: 1.5 g

Miami Chicken Wings

Preparation time: 10 minutes
Cooking time: 50 minutes
Servings: 6

Ingredients:

- 3 pounds chicken wings, at room temperature

For the Marinade:

- 1 ½ teaspoon minced garlic
- 2 teaspoons ground black pepper
- 3 limes, juiced
- 2 teaspoons lime zest
- ¼ cup hot sauce
- ½ cup soy sauce
- ½ cup olive oil

For the Sauce:

- ½ cup hot sauce
- 8 tablespoons butter, unsalted
- 2 scallions, chopped
- Lime wedges, for serving

Method:

1. Take a large bowl, place all the ingredients for the marinade in it and then whisk until smooth.
2. Add chicken wings, toss until well coated, and then marinate for 4 hours in the refrigerator, turning wings every hour.
3. When ready to grill, switch on the grill, go to the WiFi setting on your cell phone, and then connect with the grill by using your serial number as the password.
4. Go to the app of Green Mountain Grill, press the 'connect' button, and when connected, go to its setting and select the WiFi mode option and after few minutes, select the connect option again.
5. Prepare the grill, and for this, fill it hopper with gold blend wood pallets, go to Green Mountain Grill app, set the grill temperature to 375 degrees F, and let it preheat.
6. When the grill has preheated, open its lid, remove chicken wings from the marinade, and then place them on the pellet grill by using a tong in a single layer.
7. Shut the grill with lid and let chicken wings grill for 40 to 50 minutes or set the food temperature to 165 degrees F in the app and let it grill until the food reaches the set food temperature.

8. Meanwhile, prepare the sauce, and for this, take a small saucepan, place it over medium heat, add butter and when it melts, whisk in the hot sauce and set aside the sauce until required.
9. Once the app shows that the internal temperature of the chicken wings has reached 165 degrees F, open the grill, and then transfer to a large bowl.
10. Pour the sauce over chicken wings, toss until well coated, and then garnish with scallions.
11. Serve the chicken wings with lime wedges.

Nutrition Value:

- Calories: 1020 Cal
- Fat: 67 g
- Carbs: 50.2 g
- Protein: 48.3 g
- Fiber: 3.7 g

Cilantro Wings

Preparation time: 10 minutes
Cooking time: 18 minutes
Servings: 4

Ingredients:

- 1 ½ pounds chicken wings, at room temperature

For the Marinade:

- 8 cloves of garlic, peeled
- 1 cup chopped cilantro sprigs
- 3 tablespoons lemon zest
- ½ tablespoon of sea salt
- ½ tablespoon ground black pepper
- ½ tablespoon turmeric powder
- 2 tablespoons olive oil

Method:

1. Prepare the marinade, and for this, place all of its ingredients in a food processor and then pulse for 1 minute until smooth.
2. Tip the marinade in a large bowl, reserve 2 tablespoons of the marinade for the later use, add chicken wings, toss until well coated, and then marinate for 30 minutes.
3. When ready to grill, switch on the grill, go to the WiFi setting on your cell phone, and then connect with the grill by using your serial number as the password.
4. Go to the app of Green Mountain Grill, press the 'connect' button, and when connected, go to its setting and select the WiFi mode option and after few minutes, select the connect option again.
5. Prepare the grill, and for this, fill it hopper with gold blend wood pallets, go to Green Mountain Grill app, set the grill temperature to 400 degrees F, and let it preheat.
6. When the grill has preheated, open its lid, remove chicken wings from the marinade, and then place them on the pellet grill by using a tong in a single layer.
7. Shut the grill with lid and let chicken wings grill for 15 to 18 minutes or set the food temperature to 170 degrees F in the app and let it grill until the food reaches the set food temperature.
8. Once the app shows that the internal temperature of the chicken wings has reached 165 degrees F, open the grill, and then transfer to a dish.

9. Drizzle reserved marinade over the chicken wings and then serve.

Nutrition Value:

- Calories: 132.5 Cal
- Fat: 6 g
- Carbs: 5 g
- Protein: 15.4 g
- Fiber: 0.5 g

Chapter 4: Games

Rice Stuffed Game Hens

Preparation time: 10 minutes
Cooking time: 1 hour and 30 minutes
Servings: 2

Ingredients:

- 2 Cornish game hens, cleaned, rinsed, at room temperature
- 1 packet of long grain and wild rice, cooked, cooled
- Poultry rub, as needed
- Olive oil as needed

Method:

1. Switch on the grill, go to the WiFi setting on your cell phone, and then connect with the grill by using your serial number as the password.
2. Go to the app of Green Mountain Grill, press the 'connect' button, and when connected, go to its setting and select the WiFi mode option and after few minutes, select the connect option again.
3. Prepare the grill, and for this, fill it hopper with gold blend wood pallets, go to Green Mountain Grill app, set the grill temperature to 320 degrees F, and let it preheat.
4. Meanwhile, brush the oil on the exterior and inside of the hens, rub them with poultry seasoning, and then stuff with wild rice mixture.
5. When the grill has preheated, open its lid, place hens on the pellet grill by using a tong, shut with lid, and let it grill for 1 hour and 30 minutes or more until the skin of hens have turned golden brown.
6. When done, transfer hens to the dishes, let it rest for 10 minutes, and then serve.

Nutrition Value:

- Calories: 238.1 Cal
- Fat: 4.3 g
- Carbs: 23 g
- Protein: 25.6 g
- Fiber: 1.5 g

Whole Turkey

Preparation time: 10 minutes
Cooking time: 6 hours
Servings: 8

Ingredients:

- 1 whole turkey, giblets and neck removed, cleaned, rinsed, at room temperature
- 1 teaspoon Worcestershire sauce
- 1 cup apple juice
- 5 gallons of pale for brining
- Poultry rub as needed

Method:

1. Brine the turkey, and for this, take a large container, place turkey in it, and then pour in the brine.
2. Cover the container with the lid and then let it soak for overnight in the refrigerator.
3. Then remove the turkey from the brine, rinse well, and pat dry with paper towels.
4. Rub poultry rub underneath the skin of the turkey and then place it in a large disposable aluminum pan.
5. Combine apple juice and Worcestershire sauce in a spray bottle and spritz the turkey with it.
6. Switch on the grill, go to the WiFi setting on your cell phone, and then connect with the grill by using your serial number as the password.
7. Go to the app of Green Mountain Grill, press the 'connect' button, and when connected, go to its setting and select the WiFi mode option and after few minutes, select the connect option again.
8. Prepare the grill, and for this, fill it hopper with gold blend wood pallets, go to Green Mountain Grill app, set the grill temperature to 275 degrees F, and let it preheat.
9. When the grill has preheated, open its lid, place turkey on the pellet grill, shut with lid and then cook it for 15 minutes per pound.
10. Then turn the turkey over, shut with the lid, set the food temperature to 160 degrees F in the app and let it grill until the food reaches the set food temperature
11. Once the app shows that the internal temperature of the turkey has reached 160 degrees F, open the grill, and then transfer to a cutting board.

12. Cover the turkey with aluminum foil, let it rest for 30 minutes, and then carve it in pieces.
13. Serve straight away.

Nutrition Value:

- Calories: 250 Cal
- Fat: 5 g
- Carbs: 31 g
- Protein: 18 g
- Fiber: 5 g

Duck

Preparation time: 10 minutes
Cooking time: 2 hours and 30 minutes
Servings: 4

Ingredients:

- 1 whole wild duck, cleaned, rinsed
- 1 medium apple, cored, quartered
- 1 medium white onion, peeled, quartered
- Wild game rub as needed

Method:

1. Switch on the grill, go to the WiFi setting on your cell phone, and then connect with the grill by using your serial number as the password.
2. Go to the app of Green Mountain Grill, press the 'connect' button, and when connected, go to its setting and select the WiFi mode option and after few minutes, select the connect option again.
3. Prepare the grill, and for this, fill it hopper with gold blend wood pallets, go to Green Mountain Grill app, set the grill temperature to 350 degrees F, and let it preheat.
4. Meanwhile, prepare the duck, and for this, rub it with the wild game rub inside and out and then stuff the cavity with apple and onion pieces.
5. When the grill has preheated, open its lid, place duck on the pellet grill, shut with lid, and let it grill for 25 minutes per pound or until the internal temperature of the duck reach to 165 degrees F.
6. Once the app shows that the internal temperature of the chicken has reached 165 degrees F, open the grill, and then transfer the duck to a cutting.
7. Let the duck rest for 15 minutes, carve it into pieces, and then serve.

Nutrition Value:

- Calories: 269 Cal
- Fat: 21.4 g
- Carbs: 5 g
- Protein: 14.3 g
- Fiber: 2 g

Honey and Jalapeno Turkey

Preparation time: 10 minutes
Cooking time: 7 hours
Servings: 4

Ingredients:

- 1 turkey, about 12 to 20 pounds
- Sea salt as needed
- Ground black pepper as needed
- Olive oil as needed

For the Glaze:

- 1 small red onion, peeled, chopped
- 2 small apples, peeled, chopped
- 1 jalapeno, chopped
- 1 ½ cup brown sugar
- 3 tablespoons honey
- 3 tablespoons chopped sage
- 2 tablespoons olive oil
- ¾ cup apple cider vinegar

Method:

1. Switch on the grill, go to the WiFi setting on your cell phone, and then connect with the grill by using your serial number as the password.
2. Go to the app of Green Mountain Grill, press the 'connect' button, and when connected, go to its setting and select the WiFi mode option and after few minutes, select the connect option again.
3. Prepare the grill, and for this, fill it hopper with gold blend wood pallets, go to Green Mountain Grill app, set the grill temperature to 150 degrees F, and let it preheat.
4. Meanwhile, prepare the turkey, and for this, take a large disposable aluminum tray and place turkey in it.
5. When the grill has preheated, open its lid, place the tray containing turkey on the pellet grill, shut with lid, and let it grill for 20 minutes.
6. Meanwhile, prepare the glaze, and for this, take a medium saucepan, place it over medium heat, add oil and when hot, add apple, onion, and jalapeno and then cook for 4 minutes.
7. Add remaining ingredients for the glaze in the pan except for sage, stir until mixed and cook for 10 minutes until apple has turned soft.
8. Transfer the mixture into a blender, add sage and then pulse at high speed until smooth.

9. Then remove the tray containing turkey from the grill, brush it generously with oil until covered completely, and then season with salt and black pepper.
10. Return turkey into the grill, switch the temperature to 450 degrees F, and continue grilling for 1 hour or until the skin of turkey turns golden brown.
11. Then remove the tray containing turkey, brush it generously with the glaze and return turkey on the grill.
12. Switch the grill temperature to 225 degrees F and then continue grilling for 4 to 5 hours until the internal temperature reaches 165 degrees F.
13. Once the app shows that the internal temperature of the chicken has reached 165 degrees F, open the grill, and then transfer to a cutting board.
14. Cover the turkey with aluminum foil, let it rest for 30 minutes, and then carve it in pieces.
15. Serve straight away.

Nutrition Value:

- Calories: 250 Cal
- Fat: 2 g
- Carbs: 8 g
- Protein: 48 g
- Fiber: 1 g

Venison Poppers

Preparation time: 15 minutes
Cooking time: 20 minutes
Servings: 7

Ingredients:

- 1 pound regular-cut bacon
- Sea salt as needed
- 2 pounds venison steak
- Ground black pepper as needed
- 6 ounces cream cheese, softened
- 2 cups shredded cheddar cheese

Method:

1. Switch on the grill, go to the WiFi setting on your cell phone, and then connect with the grill by using your serial number as the password.
2. Go to the app of Green Mountain Grill, press the 'connect' button, and when connected, go to its setting and select the WiFi mode option and after few minutes, select the connect option again.
3. Prepare the grill, and for this, fill it hopper with gold blend wood pallets, go to Green Mountain Grill app, set the grill temperature to 400 degrees F, and let it preheat.
4. Meanwhile, cut the venison steaks into thin strips, and then season with salt and black pepper.
5. Cut bacon strips into half, then place a venison strip on a bacon slice, and top with a tablespoon of cream cheese.
6. Sprinkle cheese over cream cheese, roll it up, then secure with a toothpick and repeat with the remaining venison strips.
7. When the grill has preheated, open its lid, place venison poppers on the pellet grill by using a tong, shut with lid, and let it grill for 10 minutes per side until the bacon turns crispy.
8. Serve immediately.

Nutrition Value:

- Calories: 307.8 Cal
- Fat: 26.3 g
- Carbs: 5.1 g
- Protein: 12.7 g
- Fiber: 0.3 g

Venison Ham

Preparation time: 10 minutes
Cooking time: 3 hours
Servings: 2

Ingredients:

- 1-pound venison roast

For the Brine:

- 1 teaspoon curing salt
- ½ cup of salt
- 1 teaspoon ground cinnamon
- 1 teaspoon dried thyme
- ¼ cup brown sugar
- ½ teaspoon ground nutmeg
- ¼ cup molasses
- ½ gallon water

Method:

1. Prepare the brine, and for this, take a large pot, place it over high heat, place all the ingredients in it, stir until mixed, and then bring it to a boil.
2. Remove the pot from heat, let the brine cool completely, add venison and let it soak for 6 days.
3. Then remove the venison from the brine, rinse well, pat dry with paper towels and let it dry in the open air on a plate for 2 hours.
4. When ready to grill, switch on the grill, go to the WiFi setting on your cell phone, and then connect with the grill by using your serial number as the password.
5. Go to the app of Green Mountain Grill, press the 'connect' button, and when connected, go to its setting and select the WiFi mode option and after few minutes, select the connect option again.
6. Prepare the grill, and for this, fill it hopper with gold blend wood pallets, go to Green Mountain Grill app, set the grill temperature to 180 degrees F, and let it preheat.
7. When the grill has preheated, open its lid, place venison on the pellet grill by using a tong, shut with lid, and let it grill for 1 hour and 30 minutes.
8. Switch the temperature to 275 degrees F and continue grilling the venison until the internal temperature reaches 180 degrees F.
9. Once the app shows that the internal temperature of the chicken has reached 180 degrees F, open the grill and then transfer venison ham to a cutting board.

10. Let the venison rest for 20 minutes, cut it into slices, and then serve.

Nutrition Value:

- Calories: 178 Cal
- Fat: 3.6 g
- Carbs: 0 g
- Protein: 34.1 g
- Fiber: 0 g

Venison Steak

Preparation time: 10 minutes
Cooking time: 15 minutes
Servings: 8

Ingredients:

- 2 pounds venison steak, at room temperature
- Salt as needed
- Beef rub as needed
- Ground black pepper as needed
- Butter, unsalted, as needed

Method:

1. Switch on the grill, go to the WiFi setting on your cell phone, and then connect with the grill by using your serial number as the password.
2. Go to the app of Green Mountain Grill, press the 'connect' button, and when connected, go to its setting and select the WiFi mode option and after few minutes, select the connect option again.
3. Prepare the grill, and for this, fill it hopper with gold blend wood pallets, go to Green Mountain Grill app, set the grill temperature to 450 degrees F, and let it preheat.
4. Meanwhile, prepare the venison steaks, and for this, season them with salt, black pepper, and beef rub.
5. When the grill has preheated, open its lid, place venison steaks on the pellet grill by using a tong, top with butter, shut with lid and let it grill for 7 minutes or more until cooked to the desired level.
6. Then flip the steaks, top with more butter, and continue grilling for 7 minutes or more until cooked to the desired level.
7. When done, transfer the steaks to a cutting board, let them rest for 10 minutes and then cut into slices.
8. Serve straight away.

Nutrition Value:

- Calories: 170 Cal
- Fat: 2.9 g
- Carbs: 0 g
- Protein: 33.8 g
- Fiber: 0 g

Chapter 5: Beef

Spiced Beef Long Ribs

Preparation time: 10 minutes
Cooking time: 8 hours
Servings: 8

Ingredients:

- 6 pounds beef long ribs

For the Marinade:

- 1 small white onion, peeled, chopped
- 1 cup chopped cilantro
- 2 teaspoons minced garlic
- 1 tablespoon grated ginger
- 1 hot chili, deseeded, minced
- ½ teaspoon ground allspice
- Sea salt as needed
- Ground black pepper as needed
- ½ teaspoon nutmeg
- 2 tablespoons soy sauce
- 2 tablespoons lime juice
- ¼ cup olive oil
- ¼ cup rum

Method:

1. Prepare the marinade, and for this, place all of its ingredients in a blender and then pulse until smooth.
2. Tip the marinade in a large plastic bag, add rib, seal the bag, turn it upside down to coat the ribs with the marinade and marinate for overnight in the refrigerator.
3. When ready to grill, switch on the grill, go to the WiFi setting on your cell phone, and then connect with the grill by using your serial number as the password.
4. Go to the app of Green Mountain Grill, press the 'connect' button, and when connected, go to its setting and select the WiFi mode option and after few minutes, select the connect option again.
5. Prepare the grill, and for this, fill it hopper with gold blend wood pallets, go to Green Mountain Grill app, set the grill temperature to 250 degrees F, and let it preheat.
6. When the grill has preheated, open its lid, place marinated ribs on the pellet grill by using a tong, shut with lid, and let it grill for 8 hours until tender.
7. When done, wrap the ribs in foil, let them rest for 1 hour and then serve.

Nutrition Value:

- Calories: 306.2 Cal
- Fat: 13 g
- Carbs: 9 g
- Protein: 37.2 g
- Fiber: 1.7 g

Meat Log

Preparation time: 15 minutes
Cooking time: 4 hours
Servings: 4

Ingredients:

- 2 pounds ground beef
- ¼ of medium red onion, peeled, minced
- 5 cloves of garlic, chopped
- 1 cup chopped shiitake mushrooms
- 2 teaspoons onion powder
- 2 teaspoons garlic powder
- 1 tablespoon salt
- 1 tablespoon paprika
- 3 teaspoons ground black pepper
- 2 teaspoons cayenne powder
- ½ cup chopped cilantro
- 5 slices of cheddar cheese
- 1 egg
- ½ cup BBQ sauce

Method:

1. Switch on the grill, go to the WiFi setting on your cell phone, and then connect with the grill by using your serial number as the password.
2. Go to the app of Green Mountain Grill, press the 'connect' button, and when connected, go to its setting and select the WiFi mode option and after few minutes, select the connect option again.
3. Prepare the grill, and for this, fill it hopper with gold blend wood pallets, go to Green Mountain Grill app, set the grill temperature to 150 degrees F, and let it preheat.
4. Meanwhile, take a large bowl, place beef in it, add all the seasoning and egg and then stir until well combined.
5. Take a silicone mat or a piece a wax paper, place it on a working place, spread garlic pieces on it, place the beef mixture on it, and then spread it into a thin rectangle.
6. Spread onion, cilantro, mushroom, and cheese on top of the beef and then roll it like a sushi roll.
7. When the grill has preheated, open its lid, place wax paper with meat log on the pellet grill by, shut with lid and let it grill for 2 to 3 hours or set the food temperature to 110 degrees F in the app and let it grill until the food reaches the set food temperature.

8. Then remove the beef log from the grill, switch the temperature of the grill to 400 degrees F, and let it preheat.
9. Brush the meat log with BBQ sauce, return it to the grill and then continue grilling until the internal temperature reaches 145 degrees F.
10. Once the app shows that the internal temperature of the meat log has reached 145 degrees F, open the grill, and then transfer to a cutting board.
11. Let the meat log rest for 10 minutes, cut it into slices, and then serve.

Nutrition Value:

- Calories: 201.8 Cal
- Fat: 13.5 g
- Carbs: 7.1 g
- Protein: 12.2 g
- Fiber: 0.7 g

Meatballs

Preparation time: 15 minutes
Cooking time: 1 hour and 30 minutes
Servings: 4

Ingredients:

- 2 pounds of ground beef
- 3 tablespoons breadcrumbs
- 1 tablespoon salt
- 3 tablespoons beef rub
- 1 tablespoon ground black pepper
- 2 eggs

Method:

1. Switch on the grill, go to the WiFi setting on your cell phone, and then connect with the grill by using your serial number as the password.
2. Go to the app of Green Mountain Grill, press the 'connect' button, and when connected, go to its setting and select the WiFi mode option and after few minutes, select the connect option again.
3. Prepare the grill, and for this, fill it hopper with gold blend wood pallets, go to Green Mountain Grill app, set the grill temperature to 225 degrees F, and let it preheat.
4. Meanwhile, take a large bowl, place beef in it, add eggs, breadcrumbs, salt, and black pepper, stir until well mixed and then shape the mixture into twelve meatballs.
5. When the grill has preheated, open its lid, place meatballs on the pellet grill by using a tong, shut with lid, and let it grill for 1 hour and 30 minutes.
6. Serve straight away.

Nutrition Value:

- Calories: 265 Cal
- Fat: 18 g
- Carbs: 2 g
- Protein: 23 g
- Fiber: 1 g

Stuffed Meatballs

Preparation time: 15 minutes
Cooking time: 1 hour and 30 minutes
Servings: 4

Ingredients:

- 2 pounds of ground beef
- 2 jalapenos, minced
- 1 medium red onion, peeled, minced
- 3 tablespoons breadcrumbs
- 1 tablespoon salt
- 3 tablespoons beef rub
- 1 tablespoon ground black pepper
- 2 eggs
- 15 cubes of mozzarella cheese

Method:

1. Switch on the grill, go to the WiFi setting on your cell phone, and then connect with the grill by using your serial number as the password.
2. Go to the app of Green Mountain Grill, press the 'connect' button, and when connected, go to its setting and select the WiFi mode option and after few minutes, select the connect option again.
3. Prepare the grill, and for this, fill it hopper with gold blend wood pallets, go to Green Mountain Grill app, set the grill temperature to 225 degrees F, and let it preheat.
4. Meanwhile, take a large bowl, place beef in it, add onion, pepper, eggs, and breadcrumbs, add all the seasoning, and then stir until well mixed.
5. Shape the mixture into fifteen balls, press a cheese cube in each meatball, then wrap beef around it and shape it into a ball.
6. When the grill has preheated, open its lid, place meatballs on the pellet grill by using a tong, shut with lid, and let it grill for 1 hour and 30 minutes.
7. Serve straight away.

Nutrition Value:

- Calories: 132.8 Cal
- Fat: 6.5 g
- Carbs: 2.3 g
- Protein: 15.3 g
- Fiber: 0.3 g

Smoked Tri-Tip

Preparation time: 10 minutes
Cooking time: 2 hours and 30 minutes
Servings: 6

Ingredients:

- 6 pounds tri-tip roast, fat trimmed
- Beef Rub as needed
- BBQ Sauce as needed

Method:

1. Switch on the grill, go to the WiFi setting on your cell phone, and then connect with the grill by using your serial number as the password.
2. Go to the app of Green Mountain Grill, press the 'connect' button, and when connected, go to its setting and select the WiFi mode option and after few minutes, select the connect option again.
3. Prepare the grill, and for this, fill it hopper with gold blend wood pallets, go to Green Mountain Grill app, set the grill temperature to 225 degrees F, and let it preheat.
4. Meanwhile, rub the roast with beef rub and then brush generously with the BBQ sauce.
5. When the grill has preheated, open its lid, place roast on the pellet grill by using a tong, shut with lid, and let it grill for 2 hours and 30 minutes.
6. When done, wrap the roast in foil, let it rest for 10 minutes and then cut it into slices.
7. Serve straight away.

Nutrition Value:

- Calories: 392 Cal
- Fat: 22 g
- Carbs: 0.5 g
- Protein: 47 g
- Fiber: 0 g

Black Pepper Smoked Jerky

Preparation time: 10 minutes
Cooking time: 12 hours
Servings: 4

Ingredients:

- 3 pounds beef, lean, thinly sliced
- ½ cup white sugar
- 2 tablespoons ground black pepper
- 1 cup of soy sauce
- ½ cup Worcestershire sauce
- ½ cup dry white wine
- ¼ cup chipotle BBQ sauce

Method:

1. Prepare the marinade, and for this, take a medium bowl, place all the ingredients in it except for beef and then whisk until combined.
2. Pour the marinade in a large plastic bag, add beef slices, seal the bag, turn it upside down to coat it, and then let it marinate for a minimum of 3 hours in the refrigerator.
3. When ready to grill, switch on the grill, go to the WiFi setting on your cell phone, and then connect with the grill by using your serial number as the password.
4. Go to the app of Green Mountain Grill, press the 'connect' button, and when connected, go to its setting and select the WiFi mode option and after few minutes, select the connect option again.
5. Prepare the grill, and for this, fill it hopper with gold blend wood pallets, go to Green Mountain Grill app, set the grill temperature to 165 degrees F, and let it preheat.
6. When the grill has preheated, open its lid, place beef slices on the pellet grill by using a tong, shut with lid and let it grill for 6 to 12 hours until beef turn dry.
7. Serve straight away.

Nutrition Value:

- Calories: 320.3 Cal
- Fat: 4 g
- Carbs: 24 g
- Protein: 48 g
- Fiber: 4 g

Steaks

Preparation time: 10 minutes
Cooking time: 40
Servings: 4

Ingredients:

- 1-pound steaks, at room temperature
- Beef rub as needed
- Sizzle rub as needed
- Baste mix as needed
- ½ cup apple juice
- 3 tablespoons Worcestershire sauce

Method:

1. Switch on the grill, go to the WiFi setting on your cell phone, and then connect with the grill by using your serial number as the password.
2. Go to the app of Green Mountain Grill, press the 'connect' button, and when connected, go to its setting and select the WiFi mode option and after few minutes, select the connect option again.
3. Prepare the grill, and for this, fill it hopper with gold blend wood pallets, go to Green Mountain Grill app, set the grill temperature to 450 degrees F, and let it preheat.
4. Meanwhile, prepare the steaks, and for this, rub each steal with beef rub, sizzle rub and baste mix.
5. Combine apple juice and Worcestershire sauce in a small spray bottle and then spray it well over steaks.
6. When the grill has preheated, open its lid, place steaks on the pellet grill by using a tong, shut with lid, and let it grill for 15 to 20 minutes per side until cooked to desired doneness.
7. When done, let steaks cool for 10 minutes, then cut into slices and serve.

Nutrition Value:

- Calories: 614 Cal
- Fat: 41 g
- Carbs: 0 g
- Protein: 58 g
- Fiber: 0 g

Beef Brisket

Preparation time: 10 minutes
Cooking time: 16 hours
Servings: 8

Ingredients:

- 7 to 10 pounds Beef Brisket, fat trimmed, at room temperature
- Beef rub as needed
- Ground black pepper as needed
- Salt as needed
- 1 cup apple juice
- 6 tablespoons Worcestershire sauce

Method:

1. Score 3/8-inches square on brisket, then rub with beef rub, salt, and black pepper and then marinate for a minimum of 6 hours in the refrigerator.
2. When ready to grill, switch on the grill, go to the WiFi setting on your cell phone, and then connect with the grill by using your serial number as the password.
3. Go to the app of Green Mountain Grill, press the 'connect' button, and when connected, go to its setting and select the WiFi mode option and after few minutes, select the connect option again.
4. Prepare the grill, and for this, fill it hopper with gold blend wood pallets, go to Green Mountain Grill app, set the grill temperature to 185 degrees F, and let it preheat.
5. Pour ½ cup apple juice in a small spray bottle, add 3 tablespoons Worcestershire sauce, and then shake until combined.
6. When the grill has preheated, open its lid, place brisket fat-side-up on the pellet grill, spray with apple juice mixture, shut with lid, and let it grill for 5 hours.
7. Then turn over the brisket, spray with the apple juice mixture and continue grilling for 2 hours or until the internal temperature of brisket reaches to 165 degrees F
8. Once the app shows that the internal temperature of the chicken has reached 165 degrees F, open the grill and then transfer brisket to a cutting board.
9. Wrap brisket in aluminum foil, mix together remaining apple juice and Worcestershire sauce, pour it over brisket, and then seal it.
10. Switch the temperature of the grill to 225 degrees F, place wrapped brisket on it, and then continue grilling for 2 to 6 hours until the internal temperature reaches to 198 degrees F.

11. When done, remove brisket from the grill and let it rest for 1 hour and 30 minutes.
12. Unwrap the brisket, drain the juice and then cut it into 1/8-inch slices.
13. Serve straight away.

Nutrition Value:

- Calories: 404 Cal
- Fat: 21.2 g
- Carbs: 18.4 g
- Protein: 33.2 g
- Fiber: 0.4 g

BBQ Burger

Preparation time: 10 minutes
Cooking time: 20 minutes
Servings: 5

Ingredients:

- 2 pounds ground beef
- 1 tablespoon onion powder
- 1 tablespoon garlic powder
- 2 teaspoons salt
- 2 teaspoons ground black pepper
- 1 tablespoon beef rub
- 1 egg

Method:

1. Switch on the grill, go to the WiFi setting on your cell phone, and then connect with the grill by using your serial number as the password.
2. Go to the app of Green Mountain Grill, press the 'connect' button, and when connected, go to its setting and select the WiFi mode option and after few minutes, select the connect option again.
3. Prepare the grill, and for this, fill it hopper with gold blend wood pallets, go to Green Mountain Grill app, set the grill temperature to 500 degrees F, and let it preheat.
4. Meanwhile, prepare the patties, and for this, take a large bowl, place beef in it, and then add remaining ingredients.
5. Stir until well combined and then shape the mixture into five patties.
6. When the grill has preheated, open its lid, place burger patties on the pellet grill by using a tong, shut with lid, and let it grill for 7 to 10 minutes per side until cooked.
7. When done, assemble patties as a burger with favorite toppings like bacon, onions, and lettuce and serve with a favorite dip.

Nutrition Value:

- Calories: 323 Cal
- Fat: 23 g
- Carbs: 1 g
- Protein: 26 g
- Fiber: 0 g

Smoked Prime Rib

Preparation time: 10 minutes
Cooking time: 5 hours
Servings: 4

Ingredients:

- 5 pounds prime rib roast
- 1 cup beef rub
- 1 tablespoon Worcestershire sauce
- 1 tablespoon soy sauce
- 1 tablespoon olive oil
- ¼ cup of water

Method:

1. Take a small bowl, place beef rub in it and then whisk on Worcestershire sauce, soy sauce, oil, and water until combined.
2. Brush this mixture generously on all sides of the roast and then let it rest for 2 hours at room temperature.
3. When ready to grill, switch on the grill, go to the WiFi setting on your cell phone, and then connect with the grill by using your serial number as the password.
4. Go to the app of Green Mountain Grill, press the 'connect' button, and when connected, go to its setting and select the WiFi mode option and after few minutes, select the connect option again.
5. Prepare the grill, and for this, fill it hopper with gold blend wood pallets, go to Green Mountain Grill app, set the grill temperature to 400 degrees F, and let it preheat.
6. When the grill has preheated, open its lid, place roast on the pellet grill by using a tong, shut with lid, let it grill for 1 hour, then switch the temperature to 225 degrees F and continue cooking until the internal temperature of roast reach to 125 degrees F.
7. Once the app shows that the internal temperature of the chicken has reached 125 degrees F, open the grill, transfer roast to a cutting board and let it rest for 30 minutes.
8. Serve straight away.

Nutrition Value:

- Calories: 323 Cal
- Fat: 23 g
- Carbs: 1 g
- Protein: 26 g
- Fiber: 0 g

Brats

Preparation time: 10 minutes
Cooking time: 20 minutes
Servings: 6

Ingredients:

- 6 beef sausages

Method:

1. Switch on the grill, go to the WiFi setting on your cell phone, and then connect with the grill by using your serial number as the password.
2. Go to the app of Green Mountain Grill, press the 'connect' button, and when connected, go to its setting and select the WiFi mode option and after few minutes, select the connect option again.
3. Prepare the grill, and for this, fill it hopper with gold blend wood pallets, go to Green Mountain Grill app, set the grill temperature to 450 degrees F, and let it preheat.
4. When the grill has preheated, open its lid, place sausages on the pellet grill by using a tong, shut with lid and let it grill for 10 minutes per side or set the food temperature to 155 degrees F in the app and let it grill until the food reaches the set food temperature.
5. Once the app shows that the internal temperature of the chicken has reached 165 degrees F, open the grill and then transfer sausages to a dish.
6. Let the sausages rest for 10 minutes, and then serve.

Nutrition Value:

- Calories: 143 Cal
- Fat: 12 g
- Carbs: 0.2 g
- Protein: 7.8 g
- Fiber: 0 g

Chapter 6: Pork

Pork Belly Burnt Ends

Preparation time: 10 minutes
Cooking time: 5 hours
Servings: 4

Ingredients:

- 1 Pork belly slab
- BBQ pork rub as needed
- BBQ sauce as needed

Method:

1. Cut the pork belly into 1-inch long strips, starting from the skinless side, and then place the strips in a large bowl.
2. Add rub, toss until coated, and then let it marinate for a minimum of 30 minutes in the refrigerator.
3. When ready to grill, switch on the grill, go to the WiFi setting on your cell phone, and then connect with the grill by using your serial number as the password.
4. Go to the app of Green Mountain Grill, press the 'connect' button, and when connected, go to its setting and select the WiFi mode option and after few minutes, select the connect option again.
5. Prepare the grill, and for this, fill it hopper with apple blend wood pallets, go to Green Mountain Grill app, set the grill temperature to 250 degrees F, and let it preheat.
6. When the grill has preheated, open its lid, place pork belly strips on the pellet grill by using a tong, shut with lid and let it grill for 3 to 4 hours or set the food temperature to 198 degrees F in the app and let it grill until the food reaches the set food temperature.
7. Once the app shows that the internal temperature of the pork has reached 198 degrees F, open the grill and then transfer pork strips to a cutting board.
8. Let pork cool for 15 minutes, then cut them into 1-inch cubes and place them in a disposable aluminum foil tray.
9. Add BBQ sauce, toss until well coated, cover the tray with foil, return it on the grill and continue grilling for 1 hour.
10. Serve straight away.

Nutrition Value:

- Calories: 300 Cal
- Fat: 13 g
- Carbs: 21 g
- Protein: 26 g
- Fiber: 1 g

Beer Brats

Preparation time: 10 minutes
Cooking time: 3 hours
Servings: 6

Ingredients:

- 6 uncooked German brats
- 1 medium sweet onion, peeled, chopped into thick slices
- 3 tablespoons brown sugar
- 8 ounces butter, salted, cut into 8 pieces
- 22 ounces amber ale

Method:

1. Switch on the grill, go to the WiFi setting on your cell phone, and then connect with the grill by using your serial number as the password.
2. Go to the app of Green Mountain Grill, press the 'connect' button, and when connected, go to its setting and select the WiFi mode option and after few minutes, select the connect option again.
3. Prepare the grill, and for this, fill it hopper with apple blend wood pallets, go to Green Mountain Grill app, set the grill temperature to 250 degrees F, and let it preheat.
4. Meanwhile, take a large pan, scatter onion in its bottom, sprinkle with sugar, top with butter slices and sausages, and then pour ale over the sausages.
5. When the grill has preheated, open its lid, place the pan on the pellet grill by using a tong, shut with lid, and let it grill for 3 hours until thoroughly cooked.
6. Serve straight away.

Nutrition Value:

- Calories: 230.4 Cal
- Fat: 21 g
- Carbs: 2 g
- Protein: 12 g
- Fiber: 0.4 g

Cherry Chipotle Ribs

Preparation time: 10 minutes
Cooking time: 6 hours
Servings: 4

Ingredients:

- 1 large rack of baby back ribs, membrane removed, at room temperature
- ½ cup brown sugar
- 2 tablespoons mustard paste
- Pork rub as needed
- 2 tablespoons butter, unsalted
- 3 tablespoons honey
- Cherry chipotle sauce as needed

Method:

1. Switch on the grill, go to the WiFi setting on your cell phone, and then connect with the grill by using your serial number as the password.
2. Go to the app of Green Mountain Grill, press the 'connect' button, and when connected, go to its setting and select the WiFi mode option and after few minutes, select the connect option again.
3. Prepare the grill, and for this, fill it hopper with Texas blend wood pallets, go to Green Mountain Grill app, set the grill temperature to 225 degrees F, and let it preheat.
4. Meanwhile, prepare the ribs, and for this, rub with mustard paste and then sprinkle with pork rub until coated on all sides.
5. When the grill has preheated, open its lid, place ribs on the pellet grill, shut with lid, and let it grill for 2 hours.
6. Then take a large piece of foil, place ribs on it, spread butter and honey on top, sprinkle with sugar, wrap the ribs and then continue grilling for 2 hours or until tender.
7. Then remove ribs from the grill, unwrap it, and spread evenly with chipotle sauce.
8. Switch the temperature of the grill to 275 degrees F, return the ribs on the grill and continue grilling for 1 hour or 1 hour and 30 minutes until done.
9. Let the ribs rest for 15 minutes and then serve.

Nutrition Value:

- Calories: 292.5 Cal
- Fat: 17 g
- Carbs: 20 g
- Protein: 13 g
- Fiber: 2 g

Sweet Espresso Ribs

Preparation time: 10 minutes
Cooking time: 6 hours
Servings: 6

Ingredients:

- 1 large rack of baby back ribs, membrane removed, at room temperature
- ½ cup brown sugar
- ½ cup ground espresso beans
- 3 tablespoons ground black pepper
- 2 tablespoons olive oil
- 2 tablespoons butter, unsalted, cubed
- BBQ sauce as needed

Method:

1. Switch on the grill, go to the WiFi setting on your cell phone, and then connect with the grill by using your serial number as the password.
2. Go to the app of Green Mountain Grill, press the 'connect' button, and when connected, go to its setting and select the WiFi mode option and after few minutes, select the connect option again.
3. Prepare the grill, and for this, fill it hopper with Texas blend wood pallets, go to Green Mountain Grill app, set the grill temperature to 225 degrees F, and let it preheat.
4. Meanwhile, brush ribs with oil, then stir together sugar, espresso, and black pepper and sprinkle this mixture on ribs until coated on all sides.
5. When the grill has preheated, open its lid, place ribs on the pellet grill by using a tong, shut with lid, and let it grill for 2 hours.
6. Then take a large piece of foil, place ribs on it, spread butter cubes on top, sprinkle with remaining espresso mixture, wrap the ribs and then continue grilling for 2 hours or until tender.
7. Then remove ribs from the grill, unwrap it, and spread evenly with sauce.
8. Return the ribs on the grill and then continue grilling for 1 hour or 1 hour and 30 minutes until done.
9. Let the ribs rest for 15 minutes, and then serve.

Nutrition Value:

- Calories: 416 Cal
- Fat: 21 g
- Carbs: 35 g
- Protein: 22 g
- Fiber: 1 g

BBQ Pulled Pork

Preparation time: 20 minutes
Cooking time: 15 hours
Servings: 7

Ingredients:

- 7 to 10 pounds pork butt, fat trimmed, at room temperature
- ½ cup apple cider vinegar
- Sea salt as needed
- Ground black pepper as needed
- ½ cup apple juice

For the Marinate:

- 2 tablespoons red pepper flakes
- 2 tablespoons onion powder
- 1 cup brown sugar
- 3 tablespoons paprika
- 5 tablespoons mustard paste
- 8 tablespoons olive oil

Method:

1. Prepare the marinade, and for this, take a medium bowl, place all the ingredients in it and then whisk until well combined.
2. Rub the marinade on all sides of pork butt and then let it marinate for 12 to 24 hours in the refrigerator.
3. Then switch on the grill, go to the WiFi setting on your cell phone, and then connect with the grill by using your serial number as the password.
4. Go to the app of Green Mountain Grill, press the 'connect' button, and when connected, go to its setting and select the WiFi mode option and after few minutes, select the connect option again.
5. Prepare the grill, and for this, fill it hopper with gold blend wood pallets, go to Green Mountain Grill app, set the grill temperature to 380 degrees F, and let it preheat.
6. Meanwhile, remove pork putt from the refrigerator, bring it to room temperature and then season it well with salt and black pepper.
7. When the grill has preheated, open its lid, place pork butt fat-side-up on the pellet grill, shut with lid, and let it grill for 1 hour.
8. Meanwhile, pour apple juice in a small spray bottle, add apple cider vinegar, and then shake well.

9. Switch the temperature of the grill to 225 degrees F, spray with the apple juice mixture and then continue grilling for 5 hours or until the internal temperature reaches 160 degrees F.
10. Return pork butt from the grill, place it on a large piece of foil, spray with apple juice mixture, wrap it with foil and then continue grilling the pork until the internal temperature reaches 195 degrees F.
11. Once the app shows that the internal temperature of the chicken has reached 195 degrees F, open the grill and then transfer wrapped pork to a cutting board.
12. Let the pork rest for 30 minutes, uncover it, and then shred it by using two forks.
13. Serve straight away.

Nutrition Value:

- Calories: 484 Cal
- Fat: 21.6 g
- Carbs: 46.2 g
- Protein: 26.2 g
- Fiber: 10.4 g

Baby Back Ribs

Preparation time: 10 minutes
Cooking time: 9 hours
Servings: 6

Ingredients:

- 2 racks of baby back ribs, membrane removed, at room temperature
- Cherry chipotle sauce as needed
- For the Marinade:
- 2 tablespoons minced garlic
- 1 teaspoon onion powder
- 2 teaspoons ground black pepper
- 1 tablespoon brown sugar
- 1 cup soy sauce
- 2 tablespoons red wine vinegar
- ¼ cup olive oil
- ½ teaspoon Tabasco sauce
- ¼ cup white wine

Method:

1. Take a small bowl, place all the ingredients for the marinade in it and then whisk until combined.
2. Pour the marinade in a large plastic bag, add ribs, seal the bag, turn it upside down to coat ribs with the marinade and then let it marinate for a minimum of 4 hours.
3. When ready to grill, switch on the grill, go to the WiFi setting on your cell phone, and then connect with the grill by using your serial number as the password.
4. Go to the app of Green Mountain Grill, press the 'connect' button, and when connected, go to its setting and select the WiFi mode option and after few minutes, select the connect option again.
5. Prepare the grill, and for this, fill it hopper with gold blend wood pallets, go to Green Mountain Grill app, set the grill temperature to 165 degrees F, and let it preheat.
6. When the grill has preheated, open its lid, place ribs on the pellet grill by using a tong, shut with lid, and let it grill for 4 to 6 hours, turning halfway through.
7. Switch the temperature to 225 degrees F, continue grilling for 2 hours, then brush with chipotle sauce and continue grilling for 1 hour until glazed.
8. When done, let ribs rest for 30 minutes, then cut it into slices and serve.

Nutrition Value:

- Calories: 668 Cal
- Fat: 45 g
- Carbs: 13 g
- Protein: 48 g
- Fiber: 0.3 g

Pork Chops

Preparation time: 10 minutes
Cooking time: 4 hours
Servings: 2

Ingredients:

- 1 pound pork chops, bone-in, about 1-inch thick, at room temperature
- Pork rub as needed
- Pork marinade as needed

Method:

1. Season pork chops with pork rub, place them in a large plastic bag and then pour in the marinade.
2. Seal the bag, turn it upside down and then let it marinate for a minimum of 4 hours.
3. When ready to grill, switch on the grill, go to the WiFi setting on your cell phone, and then connect with the grill by using your serial number as the password.
4. Go to the app of Green Mountain Grill, press the 'connect' button, and when connected, go to its setting and select the WiFi mode option and after few minutes, select the connect option again.
5. Prepare the grill, and for this, fill it hopper with gold blend wood pallets, go to Green Mountain Grill app, set the grill temperature to 400 degrees F, and let it preheat.
6. When the grill has preheated, open its lid, place pork chops on the pellet grill by using a tong, shut with lid, then set the food temperature to 165 degrees F in the app and let it grill until the food reaches the set food temperature.
7. Once the app shows that the internal temperature of the pork chops has reached 165 degrees F, open the grill, and then transfer to a dish.
8. Let the pork chops rest for 10 minutes, and then serve.

Nutrition Value:

- Calories: 360 Cal
- Fat: 16 g
- Carbs: 2 g
- Protein: 42 g
- Fiber: 1 g

Chapter 7: Lamb

Mustard Glazed Lamb

Preparation time: 10 minutes
Cooking time: 2 hours
Servings: 2

Ingredients:

- 6 pounds leg of lamb, semi-boneless, fat trimmed, at room temperature
- Meat rub to taste

For the Glaze:

- 10 ounces apricot spread
- 1 teaspoon garlic powder
- ¼ cup horseradish mustard

Method:

1. Switch on the grill, go to the WiFi setting on your cell phone, and then connect with the grill by using your serial number as the password.
2. Go to the app of Green Mountain Grill, press the 'connect' button, and when connected, go to its setting and select the WiFi mode option and after few minutes, select the connect option again.
3. Prepare the grill, and for this, fill it hopper with gold blend wood pallets, go to Green Mountain Grill app, set the grill temperature to 400 degrees F, and let it preheat.
4. Meanwhile, prepare the leg of lamb, and for this, season it with meat rub generously.
5. When the grill has preheated, open its lid, place the lamb on the pellet grill by using a tong, shut with lid, and let it grill for 30 minutes.
6. Meanwhile, prepare the glaze, and for this, take a small saucepan, place all of the ingredients in it and stir until combined.
7. Place the pan over medium heat, bring it to simmer, and then cook for 5 minutes, set aside until required.
8. Then switch temperature of the grill to 350 degrees F, brush lamb with the glaze until coated on all sides, grill it for 1 hour or more until the app shows the internal temperature of 145 degrees F.

9. Once the app shows that the internal temperature of the lamb has reached 145 degrees F, open the grill, then transfer to a cutting board and then wrap in the foil.
10. Let the lamb rest for 20 minutes, then cut it into slices and serve.

Nutrition Value:

- Calories: 214.4 Cal
- Fat: 12.4 g
- Carbs: 1.1 g
- Protein: 23.4 g
- Fiber: 0.1 g

Lamb Kabob

Preparation time: 10 minutes
Cooking time: 30 minutes
Servings: 4

Ingredients:

- 1 leg of lamb, boneless, fat trimmed, at room temperature
- 1 large red onion, peeled, diced
- 5 cloves of garlic, peeled
- ¼ cup parsley leaves
- 1 tablespoon wild game rub
- 1 tablespoon ground black pepper
- 1 cup olive oil
- 1 cup sherry

Method:

1. Prepare the lamb, and for this, cut it into 1 ½-inch cube, place them in a large bowl, and then season with game rub, set aside until required.
2. Take a separate bowl, place onion pieces in it, add parsley leaves, and then toss until mixed.
3. Add garlic cloves in a blender, add oil, sherry, and black pepper and then pulse at high speed until frothy.
4. Add garlic mixture to onions, toss until mixed, then add this mixture over lamb mixture, toss until mixed and let it marinate for a minimum of 8 hours in the refrigerator.
5. When ready to grill, switch on the grill, go to the WiFi setting on your cell phone, and then connect with the grill by using your serial number as the password.
6. Go to the app of Green Mountain Grill, press the 'connect' button, and when connected, go to its setting and select the WiFi mode option and after few minutes, select the connect option again.
7. Prepare the grill, and for this, fill it hopper with gold blend wood pallets, go to Green Mountain Grill app, set the grill temperature to 380 degrees F, and let it preheat.
8. Meanwhile, prepare the skewers, and for this, thread lamb pieces and onion pieces alternately.
9. When the grill has preheated, open its lid, place the lamb skewers on the pellet grill by using a tong, shut with lid, and let it grill for 10 to 15 minutes per side until cooked.

10. Serve straight away.

Nutrition Value:

- Calories: 287 Cal
- Fat: 12 g
- Carbs: 10 g
- Protein: 32 g
- Fiber: 3 g

Rack of Lamb

Preparation time: 10 minutes
Cooking time: 25 minutes
Servings: 6

Ingredients:

- 3 racks of lamb, membrane removed, at room temperature

For the Paste:

- 12 cloves of garlic, peeled
- 1 teaspoon salt
- 2 tablespoons rosemary
- ½ teaspoon ground black pepper
- 1/3 cup olive oil

Method:

1. Switch on the grill, go to the WiFi setting on your cell phone, and then connect with the grill by using your serial number as the password.
2. Go to the app of Green Mountain Grill, press the 'connect' button, and when connected, go to its setting and select the WiFi mode option and after few minutes, select the connect option again.
3. Prepare the grill, and for this, fill it hopper with gold blend wood pallets, go to Green Mountain Grill app, set the grill temperature to 400 degrees F, and let it preheat.
4. Meanwhile, prepare the paste, and for this, place all of its ingredients in a blender, pulse until smooth and then spread the paste on all sides of the racks of lamb.
5. When the grill has preheated, open its lid, place racks of lamb on the pellet grill by using a tong, shut with lid, and let it grill for 12 minutes per side until cooked to the desired level of doneness.
6. When done, transfer racks of lamb to a cutting board, let them rest for 10 minutes, and then cut them into slices.
7. Serve straight away.

Nutrition Value:

- Calories: 335 Cal
- Fat: 26.3 g
- Carbs: 2.4 g
- Protein: 21 g
- Fiber: 0 g

Chapter 8: Seafood and Fish

Pineapple and Coconut Shrimp

Preparation time: 10 minutes
Cooking time: 20 minutes
Servings: 4

Ingredients:

- 1 ½ cups white rice, uncooked, rinsed
- 2 pounds medium shrimp, peeled, deveined, at room temperature
- 1 large bunch of green onion
- 2 large red bell peppers, destemmed, cored
- 1 lime, quartered
- 1 medium pineapple, cored, halved
- 1 tablespoon of sea salt
- 1 tablespoon grated ginger
- 1 tablespoon Sriracha sauce
- 1 ½ tablespoon sugar
- 1 tablespoon curry powder
- 2 cans of coconut milk, unsweetened, coconut cream separated
- 1 cup shredded coconut, unsweetened

Method:

1. Take a medium pot, place it over medium heat, add rice, stir in salt and sugar, pour in water and milk, and then stir until mixed.
2. Bring the mixture to a boil, then switch heat to medium-low level and simmer for 20 minutes or until the rice has absorbed all the liquid, set aside until required.
3. Switch on the grill, go to the WiFi setting on your cell phone, and then connect with the grill by using your serial number as the password.
4. Go to the app of Green Mountain Grill, press the 'connect' button, and when connected, go to its setting and select the WiFi mode option and after few minutes, select the connect option again.
5. Prepare the grill, and for this, fill it hopper with gold blend wood pallets, go to Green Mountain Grill app, set the grill temperature to 400 degrees F, and let it preheat.
6. Meanwhile, prepared red peppers and pineapple and then place the coconut in a disposable aluminum tray.
7. When the grill has preheated, open its lid, place bell peppers, pineapple, green onion, and a tray containing coconut on the pellet grill by using a tong.

8. Spread shrimps on the grill mat, shut with lid and let the vegetables and shrimps grill for 20 minutes or more until vegetables developed char marks on every side, coconut turn nicely brown and then shrimps turn pink.
9. Meanwhile, prepare the marinade, and for this, place coconut cream in a medium bowl, add salt, ginger, curry powder, and Sriracha sauce and then whisk until smooth.
10. When vegetables have charred, transfer them to a cutting board, cut them into small pieces, add them to the cooked rice mixture and stir until just mixed.
11. Transfer shrimps to the prepared marinade, add toasted coconut, and then toss until well coated.
12. Top the shrimps with the rice-vegetable mixture and then serve with lime wedges.

Nutrition Value:

- Calories: 223.8 Cal
- Fat: 2.2 g
- Carbs: 28.1 g
- Protein: 24.3 g
- Fiber: 0.9 g

Spicy Shrimp Skewers

Preparation time: 10 minutes
Cooking time: 20 minutes
Servings: 5

Ingredients:

- 20 medium shrimps, peeled, deveined, at room temperature
- ½ of orange, juice
- ½ tablespoon of sea salt
- Seafood rub as needed
- 1 lime, juiced
- ½ tablespoon ground black pepper
- 1 lemon, juiced
- 1/3 cup olive oil
- Sweet and Smokey Sauce as needed

Method:

1. Switch on the grill, go to the WiFi setting on your cell phone, and then connect with the grill by using your serial number as the password.
2. Go to the app of Green Mountain Grill, press the 'connect' button, and when connected, go to its setting and select the WiFi mode option and after few minutes, select the connect option again.
3. Prepare the grill, and for this, fill it hopper with gold blend wood pallets, go to Green Mountain Grill app, set the grill temperature to 375 degrees F, and let it preheat.
4. Meanwhile, prepare the drizzle, and for this, take a medium bowl, pour in orange, lime, and lemon juice, whisk in oil until emulsified, and then whisk in salt and black pepper.
5. Thread the shrimps on five skewers, brush with the citrus-oil mixture, and then sprinkle with seafood rub until well coated.
6. When the grill has preheated, open its lid, place shrimp skewers on the pellet grill, shut with lid, and then let it grill for 15 minutes or more until shrimp start turning pink.
7. Then brush the shrimps with the sauce and continue grilling until the app shows the internal temperature reaches 140 degrees F.
8. Once the app shows that the internal temperature of the chicken has reached 140 degrees F, open the grill and then transfer shrimps to a dish.
9. Let the shrimps rest for 10 minutes, and then serve.

Nutrition Value:

- Calories: 142.1 Cal
- Fat: 3.6 g
- Carbs: 5.7 g
- Protein: 20.8 g
- Fiber: 1.1 g

Bacon-Wrapped Shrimp

Preparation time: 10 minutes
Cooking time: 30 minutes
Servings: 4

Ingredients:

- 1-pound medium Shrimp, peeled, deveined, at room temperature
- 1 lime, juiced
- 1-pound Bacon, thin-cut
- ¼ cup pineapple juice

Method:

1. Switch on the grill, go to the WiFi setting on your cell phone, and then connect with the grill by using your serial number as the password.
2. Go to the app of Green Mountain Grill, press the 'connect' button, and when connected, go to its setting and select the WiFi mode option and after few minutes, select the connect option again.
3. Prepare the grill, and for this, fill it hopper with gold blend wood pallets, go to Green Mountain Grill app, set the grill temperature to 275 degrees F, and let it preheat.
4. When the grill has preheated, open its lid, cut bacon slices in half, spread them on the grilling mat, and then grill until almost edible.
5. Then remove bacon slices from the grill, let them cool for 5 minutes and then wipe clean the grease from the mat.
6. Prepare the shrimps, and for this, take them in a large bowl, drizzle with lime juice and pineapple juice and then toss until coated.
7. Wrap each shrimp with each slice of bacon and then secure them with a toothpick.
8. Switch the temperature of the grill to 425 degrees F, and when it preheats, place prepared shrimps on the grill and then grill for 5 to 7 minutes per side until the bacon has turned crisp and shrimps have turned pink.
9. Serve straight away.

Nutrition Value:

- Calories: 207.6 Cal
- Fat: 2 g
- Carbs: 1 g
- Protein: 23 g
- Fiber: 0 g

Shrimp Chipotle

Preparation time: 10 minutes
Cooking time: 16 minutes
Servings: 4

Ingredients:

- 1-pound medium Shrimp, peeled, deveined, at room temperature
- Chipotle sauce
- Roasted garlic chipotle rub

Method:

1. Rub the shrimps with garlic chipotle rub, thread them on five skewers, brush with chipotle sauce, and then let marinate for a minimum of 30 minutes in the refrigerator.
2. When ready to grill, switch on the grill, go to the WiFi setting on your cell phone, and then connect with the grill by using your serial number as the password.
3. Go to the app of Green Mountain Grill, press the 'connect' button, and when connected, go to its setting and select the WiFi mode option and after few minutes, select the connect option again.
4. Prepare the grill, and for this, fill it hopper with gold blend wood pallets, go to Green Mountain Grill app, set the grill temperature to 330 degrees F, and let it preheat.
5. When the grill has preheated, open its lid, place shrimp skewers on the pellet grill by using a tong, shut with lid, and let it grill for 8 minutes per side until shrimps have turned pink.
6. Serve straight away.

Nutrition Value:

- Calories: 152 Cal
- Fat: 2.8 g
- Carbs: 5.1 g
- Protein: 24.2 g
- Fiber: 0.3 g

Smoked Salmon

Preparation time: 10 minutes
Cooking time: 8 hours
Servings: 2

Ingredients:

- 2 salmon filets, skinless

For the Marinade:

- 1 teaspoon onion powder
- 2 teaspoons garlic powder
- 1 teaspoon ground black pepper
- 2 tablespoons brown sugar
- 1/8 teaspoon tabasco sauce
- 2 tablespoons apple cider vinegar
- 2 tablespoons honey
- 2 cups soy sauce

Method:

1. Prepare the marinade, and for this, take a medium bowl, place all of its ingredients in it and then whisk until combined.
2. Take a large plastic bag, pour in the marinade, add salmon fillets, seal the bag, turn it upside to coat salmon fillets with the marinade, and then marinate for a minimum of 8 hours.
3. When ready to grill, switch on the grill, go to the WiFi setting on your cell phone, and then connect with the grill by using your serial number as the password.
4. Go to the app of Green Mountain Grill, press the 'connect' button, and when connected, go to its setting and select the WiFi mode option and after few minutes, select the connect option again.
5. Prepare the grill, and for this, fill it hopper with gold blend wood pallets, go to Green Mountain Grill app, set the grill temperature to 350 degrees F, and let it preheat.
6. Meanwhile, remove salmon fillets from the marinade, pat them dry and then bring to the room temperature.
7. When the grill has preheated, open its lid, place marinated salmon filets on the pellet grill by using a tong, shut with lid, and let it grill for 5 to 8 hours until thoroughly cooked.
8. Let the salmon rest for 10 minutes and then serve.

Nutrition Value:

- Calories: 264 Cal
- Fat: 9.9 g
- Carbs: 0 g
- Protein: 42.7 g
- Fiber: 0 g

Basic Fish

Preparation time: 10 minutes
Cooking time: 5 hours
Servings: 2

Ingredients:

- 4 pounds fish like salmon, cleaned, rinsed

For the Marinade:

- ¼ cup of salt
- 3 tablespoons ground black pepper
- ¼ cup white sugar
- 1 tablespoon cayenne pepper
- ¼ cup brown sugar
- 8 cups of water

Method:

1. Clean and rinse the salmon and then cut it into 3-by-4 inches thick pieces, leave the skin on.
2. Prepare the marinade, and for this, take a medium bowl, place all of its ingredients in it and then whisk until combined.
3. Take a large plastic bag, pour in the marinade, add salmon pieces, seal the bag, turn it upside to coat salmon fillets with the marinade, and then marinate for a minimum of 4 hours.
4. When ready to grill, switch on the grill, go to the WiFi setting on your cell phone, and then connect with the grill by using your serial number as the password.
5. Go to the app of Green Mountain Grill, press the 'connect' button, and when connected, go to its setting and select the WiFi mode option and after few minutes, select the connect option again.
6. Prepare the grill, and for this, fill it hopper with gold blend wood pallets, go to Green Mountain Grill app, set the grill temperature to 175 degrees F, and let it preheat.
7. Meanwhile, remove salmon pieces from the marinade, pat them dry and then bring to room temperature.
8. When the grill has preheated, open its lid, place salmon skin-side-down on the pellet grill by using a tong, shut with lid and let it grill for 2 to 5 hours or until thoroughly cooked.

9. Once the app shows that the internal temperature of the chicken has reached 165 degrees F, open the grill, and then transfer to a dish.
10. Let the salmon rest for 10 minutes, and then serve.

Nutrition Value:

- Calories: 233 Cal
- Fat: 12 g
- Carbs: 0 g
- Protein: 25 g
- Fiber: 0 g

Salmon Steaks

Preparation time: 10 minutes
Cooking time: 15 minutes
Servings: 4

Ingredients:

- 4 salmon steaks, at room temperature

For the Sauce:

- ¼ teaspoon minced ginger
- ¼ cup brown sugar
- 3 teaspoons minced garlic
- ¼ teaspoon crushed red pepper flakes
- 3 teaspoons minced parsley
- ¼ teaspoon cayenne pepper
- ¼ cup balsamic vinegar

Method:

1. Switch on the grill, go to the WiFi setting on your cell phone, and then connect with the grill by using your serial number as the password.
2. Go to the app of Green Mountain Grill, press the 'connect' button, and when connected, go to its setting and select the WiFi mode option and after few minutes, select the connect option again.
3. Prepare the grill, and for this, fill it hopper with gold blend wood pallets, go to Green Mountain Grill app, set the grill temperature to 400 degrees F, and let it preheat.
4. Meanwhile, take a medium bowl, place all the ingredients for the sauce in it, whisk until combined, and then brush it well on skinless of salmon steaks.
5. When the grill has preheated, open its lid, place salmon steaks on the pellet grill by using a tong, shut with lid and let it grill for 5 minutes per side until fork tender.
6. Let the salmon steaks rest for 10 minutes, and then serve.

Nutrition Value:

- Calories: 468 Cal
- Fat: 28 g
- Carbs: 0 g
- Protein: 50 g
- Fiber: 0 g

Catfish Fillets

Preparation time: 10 minutes
Cooking time: 15 minutes
Servings: 4

Ingredients:

- 4 catfish fillets, at room temperature
- Fish rub as needed
- 1 lemon, juiced

Method:

1. Switch on the grill, go to the WiFi setting on your cell phone, and then connect with the grill by using your serial number as the password.
2. Go to the app of Green Mountain Grill, press the 'connect' button, and when connected, go to its setting and select the WiFi mode option and after few minutes, select the connect option again.
3. Prepare the grill, and for this, fill it hopper with gold blend wood pallets, go to Green Mountain Grill app, set the grill temperature to 400 degrees F, and let it preheat.
4. Meanwhile, coat the fillets with lemon juice and then rub with the fish rub until evenly coated.
5. When the grill has preheated, open its lid, place fish fillets on the pellet grill by using a tong, shut with lid, and let it grill for 5 minutes per side until fork tender.
6. Let the fish fillets rest for 10 minutes, and then serve.

Nutrition Value:

- Calories: 323 Cal
- Fat: 9 g
- Carbs: 0 g
- Protein: 55 g
- Fiber: 0 g

Grilled Whole Trout

Preparation time: 10 minutes
Cooking time: 4 hours
Servings: 2

Ingredients:

- 1 Whole trout, Gutted, gilled
- Some dark maple syrup for basting

For the Brine:

- Salt as needed
- 2 tablespoons soy sauce
- 2 tablespoons sugar
- 2 bay leaves
- ¼ cup whole peppercorns
- Water as needed

Method:

1. Brine the trout, and for this, place it in a large container and then pour in enough water to soak the fish completely.
2. Take out the trout from the water, stir in salt, 1 tablespoon per cup of water and remaining ingredients for the brine and then stir well until salt and sugar have dissolved.
3. Return trout into the brine mixture, cover with the lid and then let it soak for a minimum of 8 hours in the refrigerator.
4. Then remove trout from the brine, rinse well, pat dry with paper towels and let it cool in the open air for a minimum of 2 hours.
5. When ready to grill, switch on the grill, go to the WiFi setting on your cell phone, and then connect with the grill by using your serial number as the password.
6. Go to the app of Green Mountain Grill, press the 'connect' button, and when connected, go to its setting and select the WiFi mode option and after few minutes, select the connect option again.
7. Prepare the grill, and for this, fill it hopper with gold blend wood pallets, go to Green Mountain Grill app, set the grill temperature to 220 degrees F, and let it preheat.
8. When the grill has preheated, open its lid, place trout on the pellet grill by using a tong, shut with lid, and let it grill for 1 hour 30 minutes to 4 hours until cooked, the grilling time depends on the thickness of the trout.
9. Let the trout rest for 10 minutes, and then serve.

Nutrition Value:

- Calories: 246 Cal
- Fat: 2 g
- Carbs: 0 g
- Protein: 50 g
- Fiber: 0 g

Grilled Tilapia

Preparation time: 10 minutes
Cooking time: 2 hours
Servings: 6

Ingredients:

- 6 tilapia fillets, deboned
- ½ teaspoon garlic powder
- ½ teaspoon lemon pepper seasoning
- 1 teaspoon salt
- 2 tablespoons lemon juice
- 3 tablespoons olive oil

Method:

1. Switch on the grill, go to the WiFi setting on your cell phone, and then connect with the grill by using your serial number as the password.
2. Go to the app of Green Mountain Grill, press the 'connect' button, and when connected, go to its setting and select the WiFi mode option and after few minutes, select the connect option again.
3. Prepare the grill, and for this, fill it hopper with gold blend wood pallets, go to Green Mountain Grill app, set the grill temperature to 250 degrees F, and let it preheat.
4. Meanwhile, prepare the dish, and for this, take a small bowl and then add garlic powder, lemon pepper seasoning, salt, lemon juice, and oil.
5. Wisk until combined and then brush it well on all sides of the fillets.
6. When the grill has preheated, open its lid, place fillets on the pellet grill by using a tong, shut with lid, and let it grill for 2 hours or until tender.
7. Let the fillets rest for 10 minutes, and then serve.

Nutrition Value:

- Calories: 260 Cal
- Fat: 6 g
- Carbs: 2 g
- Protein: 52 g
- Fiber: 0 g

Grilled Seabass

Preparation time: 10 minutes
Cooking time: 10 minutes
Servings: 4

Ingredients:

- 2 seabass fillets, deboned, skinless
- 2 teaspoon dried tarragon
- Salt as needed
- 1 tablespoon olive oil

Method:

1. Switch on the grill, go to the WiFi setting on your cell phone, and then connect with the grill by using your serial number as the password.
2. Go to the app of Green Mountain Grill, press the 'connect' button, and when connected, go to its setting and select the WiFi mode option and after few minutes, select the connect option again.
3. Prepare the grill, and for this, fill it hopper with gold blend wood pallets, go to Green Mountain Grill app, set the grill temperature to 450 degrees F, and let it preheat.
4. Meanwhile, prepare the seabass fillets, and for this, season with salt, sprinkle with tarragon, and then brush with oil.
5. When the grill has preheated, open its lid, place seabass fillets on the pellet grill by using a tong, shut with lid and let it grill for 5 minutes per side or more until the app shows the internal temperature of 125 degrees F.
6. Let the seabass fillets rest for 10 minutes, and then serve.

Nutrition Value:

- Calories: 232 Cal
- Fat: 12 g
- Carbs: 0 g
- Protein: 28 g
- Fiber: 0 g

Chapter 9: Vegetables

Parmesan and Kale Pizza

Preparation time: 10 minutes
Cooking time: 20 minutes
Servings: 4

Ingredients:

- 1 pizza crust
- 2 cups chopped kale
- 1 tablespoon of sea salt
- 1/3 cup chopped sage
- 2 cups grated parmesan cheese
- Olive oil as needed

Method:

1. Switch on the grill, go to the WiFi setting on your cell phone, and then connect with the grill by using your serial number as the password.
2. Go to the app of Green Mountain Grill, press the 'connect' button, and when connected, go to its setting and select the WiFi mode option and after few minutes, select the connect option again.
3. Prepare the grill, and for this, fill it hopper with gold blend wood pallets, go to Green Mountain Grill app, set the grill temperature to 400 degrees F, and let it preheat.
4. Meanwhile, prepare the pizza, and for this, take four 5-by11 inches-soaked pizza grill planks, spread oil on the top and then sprinkle with cornmeal.
5. Divide the pizza crust into four sections, roll each ball into a long rectangle, and then place each crust on the prepared planks.
6. When the grill has preheated, open its lid, place pizza planks on the pellet grill, shut with lid and let it grill for 10 minutes or until the crust starts to turn golden.
7. Then scatter kale leaves on top of each crust, sprinkle with salt and sage, top with the cheese, and continue grilling for another 10 minutes until cheese has melted.
8. When done, remove prepared pizza from the grill, let it rest for 2 minutes on the pizza plank, and then serve.

Nutrition Value:

- Calories: 282 Cal
- Fat: 13 g
- Carbs: 34 g
- Protein: 6 g
- Fiber: 3 g

Watermelon Gazpacho

Preparation time: 10 minutes
Cooking time: 15 minutes
Servings: 4

Ingredients:

- 1-pound mini bell peppers
- ½ of a large watermelon, seeded, sliced in wedges
- 4 medium Roma tomatoes, cut in half
- 2 medium shallots, peeled, halved
- 3 large cucumbers, peeled, sliced lengthwise
- 5 cloves of garlic, peeled
- 1 large bunch of basil leaves
- 1 tablespoon of sea salt
- 1 teaspoon ground black pepper
- 2 tablespoons balsamic vinegar
- 3 tablespoons olive oil
- 4 tablespoons water

Method:

1. Switch on the grill, go to the WiFi setting on your cell phone, and then connect with the grill by using your serial number as the password.
2. Go to the app of Green Mountain Grill, press the 'connect' button, and when connected, go to its setting and select the WiFi mode option and after few minutes, select the connect option again.
3. Prepare the grill, and for this, fill it hopper with fruit blend wood pallets, go to Green Mountain Grill app, set the grill temperature to 350 degrees F, and let it preheat.
4. Meanwhile, prepare the vegetables and fruits and then thread cloves on skewers.
5. When the grill has preheated, open its lid, place all the vegetables and fruits on the pellet grill, shut with lid, and let it grill for 15 minutes or until slightly charred.
6. When done, transfer the vegetables and fruits to a large bowl, cool them for 15 minutes, and then transfer into a large pot.
7. Add basil and remaining ingredients and then blend by using an immersion blender until smooth.
8. Let the gazpacho chill for a minimum of 1 hour in the refrigerator and then serve.

Nutrition Value:

- Calories: 99 Cal
- Fat: 1.2 g
- Carbs: 22.2 g
- Protein: 2.4 g
- Fiber: 2.8 g

Baked Beans

Preparation time: 10 minutes
Cooking time: 2 hours and 30 minutes
Servings: 4

Ingredients:

- ¼ pound bacon
- 1 ¼ cups of navy beans, soaked, cooked
- 8 ounces crushed pineapple
- 1 small white onion, peeled, minced
- ½ teaspoon salt
- ¼ cup brown sugar
- 1 teaspoon mustard powder
- 1 teaspoon butter, unsalted
- 2 tablespoons molasses
- ¼ cup BBQ Sauce

Method:

1. Take a medium skillet pan, place it over medium heat and when hot, add bacon and then cook for 3 to 5 minutes until golden brown.
2. Transfer bacon to a large bowl, add beans, stir until combined and then set aside until required.
3. Add onion into the pan, add butter and let the onion cook for 3 minutes until tender.
4. Add salt, mustard, sugar, molasses, and BBQ sauce, stir until combined, and then bring the mixture to a boil.
5. Pour the onion mixture over beans, stir in pineapple until well combined, spoon the mixture into a disposable aluminum foil tray, and then pour in water until beans are immersed completely.
6. Then switch on the grill, go to the WiFi setting on your cell phone, and then connect with the grill by using your serial number as the password.
7. Go to the app of Green Mountain Grill, press the 'connect' button, and when connected, go to its setting and select the WiFi mode option and after few minutes, select the connect option again.
8. Prepare the grill, and for this, fill it hopper with gold blend wood pallets, go to Green Mountain Grill app, set the grill temperature to 165 degrees F, and let it preheat.

9. When the grill has preheated, open its lid, place beans in the tray on the pellet grill, shut with lid, grill for 1 hour, then switch the temperature to 325 degrees F and then continue grilling for 1 hour.
10. Serve straight away.

Nutrition Value:

- Calories: 150 Cal
- Fat: 1 g
- Carbs: 29 g
- Protein: 6 g
- Fiber: 8 g

Corn on the Cob

Preparation time: 10 minutes
Cooking time: 1 hour
Servings: 2

Ingredients:

- 2 corns on the cob

Method:

1. Place corn with their husk in a large container, cover with water, and let soak for 1 hour.
2. When ready to grill, switch on the grill, go to the WiFi setting on your cell phone, and then connect with the grill by using your serial number as the password.
3. Go to the app of Green Mountain Grill, press the 'connect' button, and when connected, go to its setting and select the WiFi mode option and after few minutes, select the connect option again.
4. Prepare the grill, and for this, fill it hopper with gold blend wood pallets, go to Green Mountain Grill app, set the grill temperature to 350 degrees F, and let it preheat.
5. When the grill has preheated, open its lid, place corn on the pellet grill by using a tong, shut with lid, and let it grill for 1 hour.
6. When done, remove corn from the grill, peel the husk and then serve.

Nutrition Value:

- Calories: 102.4 Cal
- Fat: 3.6 g
- Carbs: 17.1 g
- Protein: 3 g
- Fiber: 2.4 g

Vegetable Medley

Preparation time: 10 minutes
Cooking time: 30 minutes
Servings: 3

Ingredients:

- Mixed vegetables like red potatoes quarters, zucchini slices, eggplant slices, asparagus, cauliflower, and broccoli florets
- Yoshida marinade as needed
- Wild game rub as needed

Method:

1. Place the vegetables in a large bowl, pour in marinade, and then toss until well coated.
2. Let the vegetables marinate in the refrigerator for a minimum of 2 hours and then sprinkle with the wild game rub.
3. Switch on the grill, go to the WiFi setting on your cell phone, and then connect with the grill by using your serial number as the password.
4. Go to the app of Green Mountain Grill, press the 'connect' button, and when connected, go to its setting and select the WiFi mode option and after few minutes, select the connect option again.
5. Prepare the grill, and for this, fill it hopper with gold blend wood pallets, go to Green Mountain Grill app, set the grill temperature to 375 degrees F, and let it preheat.
6. When the grill has preheated, open its lid, place vegetables on the pellet grill by using a tong, shut with lid, and let it grill for 20 to 30 minutes until vegetables develop char marks.
7. Serve straight away.

Nutrition Value:

- Calories: 103 Cal
- Fat: 4.2 g
- Carbs: 16.3 g
- Protein: 3 g
- Fiber: 3 g

Potato Wedges

Preparation time: 10 minutes
Cooking time: 45 minutes
Servings: 4

Ingredients:

- 1-pound potatoes, cut into wedges
- 2 medium white onion, peeled, diced
- Vegetable rub as needed
- 4 tablespoons olive oil

Method:

1. Switch on the grill, go to the WiFi setting on your cell phone, and then connect with the grill by using your serial number as the password.
2. Go to the app of Green Mountain Grill, press the 'connect' button, and when connected, go to its setting and select the WiFi mode option and after few minutes, select the connect option again.
3. Prepare the grill, and for this, fill it hopper with gold blend wood pallets, go to Green Mountain Grill app, set the grill temperature to 400 degrees F, and let it preheat.
4. Meanwhile, take a large piece of foil, place potato wedges on it and then sprinkle with the rub.
5. Top the potatoes with diced onions, drizzle with oil and then wrap in foil.
6. When the grill has preheated, open its lid, place potato pack on the pellet grill by using a tong, shut with lid and let it grill for 30 to 45 minutes until cooked, shaking halfway through.
7. Serve straight away.

Nutrition Value:

- Calories: 205 Cal
- Fat: 3 g
- Carbs: 39 g
- Protein: 4 g
- Fiber: 2 g

Vegetables and Mozzarella Bowl

Preparation time: 10 minutes
Cooking time: 30 minutes
Servings: 4

Ingredients:

For the Vegetables:

- Mixed vegetables like red potatoes quarters, zucchini slices, eggplant slices, asparagus, cauliflower, and broccoli florets
- 1 ½ teaspoon salt
- ¾ teaspoon ground black pepper
- 4 tablespoons olive oil
- 4 tablespoons apple cider vinegar

For the Quinoa:

- 2 cups cooked quinoa
- 2/3 teaspoon salt
- 1/3 teaspoon ground black pepper
- 2 tablespoons chopped basil
- 1/3 cup balsamic vinegar dressing
- 1 lemon, juiced

For the Bowl:

- 2 medium avocados, peeled, pitted, diced
- Mozzarella cheese balls, bite-sized, packed in water

Method:

1. Switch on the grill, go to the WiFi setting on your cell phone, and then connect with the grill by using your serial number as the password.
2. Go to the app of Green Mountain Grill, press the 'connect' button, and when connected, go to its setting and select the WiFi mode option and after few minutes, select the connect option again.
3. Prepare the grill, and for this, fill it hopper with gold blend wood pallets, go to Green Mountain Grill app, set the grill temperature to 400 degrees F, and let it preheat.
4. Meanwhile, prepare the vegetables, and for this, place the mixed vegetables in a large bowl, add remaining ingredients and toss until well coated.
5. When the grill has preheated, open its lid, place vegetables on the pellet grill by using a tong, shut with lid, and let it grill for 20 to 30 minutes until vegetables develop char marks.

6. Meanwhile, prepare the quinoa, and for this, take a large bowl, place quinoa, add its remaining ingredients and stir until well combined, set aside until required.
7. Drain mozzarella, place them in a medium bowl, and then set aside until required.
8. When ready to assemble, divide grilled vegetables among four salad bowls, add quinoa, avocado slices, and cheese balls and then drizzle with some more balsamic dressing.
9. Serve straight away.

Nutrition Value:

- Calories: 189 Cal
- Fat: 13.5 g
- Carbs: 9.6 g
- Protein: 7.9 g
- Fiber: 1.8 g

Chapter 10: Sides and Snacks

Citrus Mimosa

Preparation time: 10 minutes
Cooking time: 20 minutes
Servings: 2

Ingredients:

- 4 whole oranges, halved
- Maple syrup as needed
- ¼ cup of sugar

Method:

1. Switch on the grill, go to the WiFi setting on your cell phone, and then connect with the grill by using your serial number as the password.
2. Go to the app of Green Mountain Grill, press the 'connect' button, and when connected, go to its setting and select the WiFi mode option and after few minutes, select the connect option again.
3. Prepare the grill, and for this, fill it hopper with gold blend wood pallets, go to Green Mountain Grill app, set the grill temperature to 350 degrees F, and let it preheat.
4. Meanwhile, cut three oranges in half and then cut the remaining orange in thin slices.
5. Brush orange halves and slices with maple syrup and then sprinkle with sugar.
6. When the grill has preheated, open its lid, place orange slices halves cut-side-down on the pellet grill by using a tong, shut with lid and let it grill for 15 to 20 minutes until slightly charred, turning every 5 minutes.
7. When done, let orange cool for 5 minutes, then juice the orange halves and pass through the strainer.
8. Divide orange juice between two champagne glasses, pour in the champagne, and then garnish with grilled orange slices.
9. Serve straight away.

Nutrition Value:

- Calories: 54.8 Cal
- Fat: 0.4 g
- Carbs: 12.5 g
- Protein: 1 g
- Fiber: 0.3 g

Jalapeno Poppers

Preparation time: 10 minutes
Cooking time: 1 hour and 15 minutes
Servings: 4

Ingredients:

- 8 slices of bacon, uncooked
- 8 jalapeno peppers
- 1 teaspoon minced garlic
- 8 ounces cream cheese, softened
- 2 slices of sourdough bread
- 1 cup shredded cheddar cheese

Method:

1. Switch on the grill, go to the WiFi setting on your cell phone, and then connect with the grill by using your serial number as the password.
2. Go to the app of Green Mountain Grill, press the 'connect' button, and when connected, go to its setting and select the WiFi mode option and after few minutes, select the connect option again.
3. Prepare the grill, and for this, fill it hopper with gold blend wood pallets, go to Green Mountain Grill app, set the grill temperature to 375 degrees F, and let it preheat.
4. Meanwhile, remove the stems of the pepper and then scrape the seeds by using a knife.
5. Take a small bowl, place cream cheese and cheese in it, add garlic, stir until well mixed and then stuff this mixture evenly into each pepper.
6. Cut the bread slices into eight squares, stuff each square in each stuffed pepper, then wrap each pepper with a bacon slice and secure with a toothpick.
7. When the grill has preheated, open its lid, place poppers on the pellet grill by using a tong, shut with lid, and let it grill for 1 hour and 15 minutes until bacon has turned crispy.
8. Serve straight away.

Nutrition Value:

- Calories: 140 Cal
- Fat: 8 g
- Carbs: 14.6 g
- Protein: 2.6 g
- Fiber: 0.6 g

Tomato and Bacon Jalapeno Poppers

Preparation time: 10 minutes
Cooking time: 25 minutes
Servings: 4

Ingredients:

- 15 jalapeno peppers
- 1 ½ cups shredded cheddar cheese

For the Filling:

- 1 cup chopped sun-dried tomato
- 8 slices of bacon, cooked, chopped
- 1 bundle of scallion, chopped
- ¼ cup basil
- 12 ounces cream cheese, softened

Method:

1. Switch on the grill, go to the WiFi setting on your cell phone, and then connect with the grill by using your serial number as the password.
2. Go to the app of Green Mountain Grill, press the 'connect' button, and when connected, go to its setting and select the WiFi mode option and after few minutes, select the connect option again.
3. Prepare the grill, and for this, fill it hopper with gold blend wood pallets, go to Green Mountain Grill app, set the grill temperature to 250 degrees F, and let it preheat.
4. Prepare the peppers, and for this, cut each pepper in half and then remove the seeds and stem.
5. Prepare the filling, and for this, take a medium bowl, place all of its ingredients in it and then stir until well combined.
6. Spoon the mixture into a plastic bag, seal it, then cut the corner, squeeze the filling into the prepared pepper halves until stuffed.
7. Sprinkle cheddar cheese on top of stuffed peppers and then arrange peppers on the cooking rack.
8. When the grill has preheated, open its lid, place the cooking rack containing peppers on the pellet grill, shut with lid and let it grill for 20 to 25 minutes until tender-crisp.
9. Serve straight away.

Nutrition Value:

- Calories: 97.8 Cal
- Fat: 7.5 g
- Carbs: 2.8 g
- Protein: 5 g
- Fiber: 0.8 g

Cilantro and Lime Grilled Corn

Preparation time: 10 minutes
Cooking time: 1 hour
Servings: 4

Ingredients:

- 4 ears of corn, husked
- 1 poblano pepper, deseeded, halved
- 3 tablespoons chopped cilantro
- 1 jalapeno pepper, deseeded, halved
- ½ teaspoon minced garlic
- ½ teaspoon salt
- ½ teaspoon ground black pepper
- ½ teaspoon paprika
- 1 tablespoon lime juice
- 1 tablespoon butter, unsalted

Method:

1. Place corn with their husk in a large container, cover with water, and let soak for 1 hour.
2. When ready to grill, switch on the grill, go to the WiFi setting on your cell phone, and then connect with the grill by using your serial number as the password.
3. Go to the app of Green Mountain Grill, press the 'connect' button, and when connected, go to its setting and select the WiFi mode option and after few minutes, select the connect option again.
4. Prepare the grill, and for this, fill it hopper with gold blend wood pallets, go to Green Mountain Grill app, set the grill temperature to 350 degrees F, and let it preheat.
5. When the grill has preheated, open its lid, place corn on the pellet grill along with pepper halves by using a tong, shut with lid, grill the corn for 1 hour and vegetables for 15 to 20 minutes until developed char marks.
6. When peppers have grilled, transfer them to a plastic bag, seal it, and let it rest for 10 minutes.
7. When done, let the corn cool for 15 minutes, then cut out the kernels, place them in a medium bowl, add butter, and then stir until it melts.
8. Remove peppers from the plastic bag, peel their charred skin, chop the pepper and then add to the bowl containing corn kernels.
9. Add remaining ingredients, stir until combined, and then serve.

Nutrition Value:

- Calories: 97.6 Cal
- Fat: 3.3 g
- Carbs: 17.4 g
- Protein: 3 g
- Fiber: 2.5 g

Potatoes with Rosemary and Paprika

Preparation time: 10 minutes
Cooking time: 35 minutes
Servings: 3

Ingredients:

- ½ pound potatoes, cut into 1-inch pieces
- 3 cloves of garlic, peeled, cut into third
- ½ of a medium white onion, peeled, cut into small chunks
- ¾ teaspoon crushed dried rosemary
- ¼ teaspoon salt
- ¼ teaspoon ground black pepper
- ¼ teaspoon smoked paprika
- ½ tablespoon and 1 teaspoon olive oil

Method:

1. Switch on the grill, go to the WiFi setting on your cell phone, and then connect with the grill by using your serial number as the password.
2. Go to the app of Green Mountain Grill, press the 'connect' button, and when connected, go to its setting and select the WiFi mode option and after few minutes, select the connect option again.
3. Prepare the grill, and for this, fill it hopper with gold blend wood pallets, go to Green Mountain Grill app, set the grill temperature to 400 degrees F, and let it preheat.
4. Meanwhile, take a large bowl, place potatoes in it, add onion and garlic, add remaining ingredients and then toss until well coated.
5. Take three large pieces of aluminum foil, divide potatoes evenly among them, wrap each foil and then seal the packets.
6. When the grill has preheated, open its lid, place potato packets on the pellet grill by using a tong, shut with li, grill for 20 minutes, then flip the packets and continue grilling for 15 minutes.
7. When done, let potatoes rest for 10 minutes, and then serve.

Nutrition Value:

- Calories: 177 Cal
- Fat: 5 g
- Carbs: 27 g
- Protein: 2 g
- Fiber: 3 g

Chapter 11: Desserts

Banana Boats

Preparation time: 10 minutes
Cooking time: 10 minutes
Servings: 4

Ingredients:

- Crushed graham crackers as needed
- 1 bunch of bananas
- 1 cup chocolate sauce
- Caramel, melted, as needed
- Chocolate chips as needed
- Small marshmallows as needed

Method:

1. Switch on the grill, go to the WiFi setting on your cell phone, and then connect with the grill by using your serial number as the password.
2. Go to the app of Green Mountain Grill, press the 'connect' button, and when connected, go to its setting and select the WiFi mode option and after few minutes, select the connect option again.
3. Prepare the grill, and for this, fill it hopper with gold blend wood pallets, go to Green Mountain Grill app, set the grill temperature to 350 degrees F, and let it preheat.
4. Meanwhile, cut the stem of each banana, open its peel from the middle by slicing down the middle but not all the way through, and then spread the ends to make a pocket.
5. Fill the pocket in each banana with marshmallow and chocolate chips and then wrap in aluminum foil.
6. When the grill has preheated, open its lid, place wrapped bananas on the pellet grill, shut with lid, and let it grill for 10 minutes.
7. Meanwhile, melt the caramel in the microwave and then set aside until required.
8. When done, unwrap the bananas, top with graham crackers, drizzle with caramel and chocolate sauce and then serve.

Nutrition Value:

- Calories: 199 Cal
- Fat: 4 g
- Carbs: 40 g
- Protein: 2 g
- Fiber: 2 g

Grilled Fruit Skewers

Preparation time: 10 minutes
Cooking time: 5 minutes
Servings: 6

Ingredients:

- 6 large strawberries
- 1 medium pineapple, destemmed, cored, cut into large chunks
- ½ cup powdered white sugar
- 1 tablespoon bourbon
- 3 tablespoons chocolate creamer

Method:

1. Switch on the grill, go to the WiFi setting on your cell phone, and then connect with the grill by using your serial number as the password.
2. Go to the app of Green Mountain Grill, press the 'connect' button, and when connected, go to its setting and select the WiFi mode option and after few minutes, select the connect option again.
3. Prepare the grill, and for this, fill it hopper with gold blend wood pallets, go to Green Mountain Grill app, set the grill temperature to 400 degrees F, and let it preheat.
4. Meanwhile, cut each berry in 3 pieces and then thread it with pineapple pieces alternately on wooden skewers.
5. When the grill has preheated, open its lid, place fruit skewers on the pellet grill and then grill for 2 to 3 minutes per side until developed char marks.
6. Prepare the glaze, and for this, place chocolate creamer in a small bowl and then whisk in sugar and bourbon until combined.
7. Drizzle the grizzle on fruit skewers and then serve.

Nutrition Value:

- Calories: 171.2 Cal
- Fat: 4 g
- Carbs: 36.2 g
- Protein: 1.4 g
- Fiber: 4.7 g

Grilled Peaches

Preparation time: 10 minutes
Cooking time: 10 minutes
Servings: 4

Ingredients:

- 4 medium peaches, halved, pitted
- 1 teaspoon cinnamon sugar
- 1/8 teaspoon salt
- 2 tablespoons sugar
- 1 stick of butter, unsalted, softened
- Olive oil as needed

Method:

1. Take a small bowl, place butter in it, stir until smooth, and then stir in salt, sugar, and cinnamon sugar until well combined.
2. Switch on the grill, go to the WiFi setting on your cell phone, and then connect with the grill by using your serial number as the password.
3. Go to the app of Green Mountain Grill, press the 'connect' button, and when connected, go to its setting and select the WiFi mode option and after few minutes, select the connect option again.
4. Prepare the grill, and for this, fill it hopper with gold blend wood pallets, go to Green Mountain Grill app, set the grill temperature to 450 degrees F, and let it preheat.
5. Prepare the peaches, and for this, cut them in half, remove it pit and then brush with oil.
6. When the grill has preheated, open its lid, place peach halves on the pellet grill by using a tong, shut with lid and then let it grill for 5 minutes per side until golden brown, just cooked and developed char marks.
7. When done, top each grilled peach with butter mixture and then serve.

Nutrition Value:

- Calories: 199 Cal
- Fat: 15.5 g
- Carbs: 17 g
- Protein: 1 g
- Fiber: 2 g

Chocolate Chip Cookies

Preparation time: 10 minutes
Cooking time: 15 minutes
Servings: 4

Ingredients:

- 2 ¼ cup all-purpose flour
- 1/3 cup white sugar
- 1 teaspoon baking soda
- ¾ cup brown sugar
- 1 teaspoon vanilla extract, unsweetened
- 1 ½ sticks butter, unsalted, softened
- 2 eggs, at room temperature
- 12 ounces of chocolate chips

Method:

1. Switch on the grill, go to the WiFi setting on your cell phone, and then connect with the grill by using your serial number as the password.
2. Go to the app of Green Mountain Grill, press the 'connect' button, and when connected, go to its setting and select the WiFi mode option and after few minutes, select the connect option again.
3. Prepare the grill, and for this, fill it hopper with gold blend wood pallets, go to Green Mountain Grill app, set the grill temperature to 375 degrees F, and let it preheat.
4. Meanwhile, prepare the cookies, and for this, take a large bowl, place flour in it and then stir in both sugars and baking soda until combined.
5. Beat in eggs until well combined and then fold in vanilla, butter, and chocolate chips until just mixed.
6. Take a large cookie sheet and then scoop the cookie mixture on it with some distance between cookies.
7. When the grill has preheated, open its lid, place cookie sheet containing cookies on the pellet grill, shut with lid, and let it grill for 10 to 15 minutes until golden brown.
8. When done, let cookies rest in the cookie sheet for 15 minutes, and then serve.

Nutrition Value:

- Calories: 444 Cal
- Fat: 22.2 g
- Carbs: 60 g
- Protein: 4.5 g
- Fiber: 1.8 g

Pineapple with Nutella

Preparation time: 10 minutes
Cooking time: 10 minutes
Servings: 4

Ingredients:

- ½ cup nuts, toasted
- 1 medium pineapple, cored
- Nutella as needed

Method:

1. Switch on the grill, go to the WiFi setting on your cell phone, and then connect with the grill by using your serial number as the password.
2. Go to the app of Green Mountain Grill, press the 'connect' button, and when connected, go to its setting and select the WiFi mode option and after few minutes, select the connect option again.
3. Prepare the grill, and for this, fill it hopper with gold blend wood pallets, go to Green Mountain Grill app, set the grill temperature to 450 degrees F, and let it preheat.
4. Meanwhile, core the pineapple and then cut it into eight to ten 1-inch thick round slices.
5. When the grill has preheated, open its lid, place pineapple slices on the pellet grill by using a tong, shut with lid and let it grill for 3 to 5 minutes per side until tender and developed char marks.
6. When done, let pineapple slices cool for 10 minutes and then spread 1 tablespoon of Nutella on top of each pineapple slice.
7. Stack pineapple slices, sprinkle with nuts, and then serve.

Nutrition Value:

- Calories: 120 Cal
- Fat: 7 g
- Carbs: 14 g
- Protein: 1 g
- Fiber: 1 g

Blackberry Crisp

Preparation time: 10 minutes
Cooking time: 45 minutes
Servings: 4

Ingredients:

For the Topping:

- 1 cup all-purpose flour
- 1 teaspoon baking powder
- 1 cup of sugar
- 1 egg, at room temperature
- 1 stick of butter, unsalted, melted

For the Filling:

- 6 cups blackberries, fresh
- ¾ cup of sugar
- 3 tablespoons cornstarch

Method:

1. Switch on the grill, go to the WiFi setting on your cell phone, and then connect with the grill by using your serial number as the password.
2. Go to the app of Green Mountain Grill, press the 'connect' button, and when connected, go to its setting and select the WiFi mode option and after few minutes, select the connect option again.
3. Prepare the grill, and for this, fill it hopper with gold blend wood pallets, go to Green Mountain Grill app, set the grill temperature to 375 degrees F, and let it preheat.
4. Meanwhile, prepare the topping, and for this, take a medium bowl, place flour in it and then stir in baking powder and sugar until combined.
5. Make a well in the center of the bowl, crack the egg in it and then mix until flour mixture resembles crumbs.
6. Prepare the filling, and for this, take a medium bowl, place sugar in it, stir in cornstarch, add berries and then toss until evenly coated.
7. Take a 9-inch baking pan, grease it with butter, place berries in it, scatter the topping mixture on top and then drizzle with butter.
8. When the grill has preheated, open its lid, place the pan on the pellet grill by, shut with lid and let it grill for 45 minutes until done.
9. Let the crisp cool for 10 minutes, and then serve it with ice cream.

Nutrition Value:
- Calories: 268 Cal
- Fat: 12 g
- Carbs: 38.9 g
- Protein: 3 g
- Fiber: 0 g

Conclusion

Green Mountain Grill's Davy Crockett Wood Pellet Grill is one of the most innovative, portable, and practical grills on the market. Just like many other types of equipment around the house, they can be controlled by your phone. It can reach up to 500 F degrees with precision control on the temperature. There is no need to flip your food around and or to stand beside the grill. It can be plugged into multiple sources without much worry. You can enjoy versatile cooking at any place using your car to drive this equipment around. It might be a little heavy for being portable, but to give the best features, it had to bulk up a little bit. If you have any problems concerning the grill features, a helpline for your questions is always present to fix your problems.

The device contains all the features that you would want in a portable grill. A major benefit is also that its cost is less than other grills, which provide even fewer features. This gives you the best value for your money. The device is efficient in the fuelwood economy, so there is cost efficiency even when cooking.

It's important to try different products and different items from time to time. You never know what might inspire you and become a big part of your character and life. Trying new things will help you live a happier and fulfilling life.

It's important to do new activities with friends and family as well. You bond with them will grow, and you all will have good memories to look back upon. Remembering old camping days with steaks and games will surely bring up a smile to your old self.

Stay happy, cook, and eat delicious meals and keep having fun with your life.

Happy Grilling!

www.ingramcontent.com/pod-product-compliance
Lightning Source LLC
Chambersburg PA
CBHW081403070526
44583CB00020B/2658